Large-Scale Policy Making

Paul R. Schulman
Mills College
Oakland, California

Elsevier · New York
New York · Oxford

Exclusive Distribution
throughout the World by
Greenwood Press, Westport,
Ct. U.S.A.

Elsevier North Holland, Inc.
52 Vanderbilt Avenue, New York, New York 10017

Distributors outside the United States and Canada.

Thomond Books
(A Division of Elsevier/North-Holland Scientific Publishers, Ltd.)
P.O. Box 85
Limerick, Ireland
© 1980 by Elsevier North Holland, Inc.

Library of Congress Cataloging in Publication Data

Schulman, Paul R.
    Large-scale policy making.

    Bibliography: p.
    Includes index.
    1. Policy sciences. 2. Public administration.
    3. Economies of scale. I. Title.
H61.S416   361.6′1   80-13942
ISBN 0-444-99075-5

Desk Editor   Louise Schreiber
Design   Edmée Froment
Mechanicals/Opening pages   José Garcia
Art rendered by   Vantage Art, Inc.
Production Manager   Joanne Jay
Compositor   Lexigraphics, Inc.
Printer   Haddon Craftsmen

Manufactured in the United States of America

To My Mother and Father

Contents

A lake allows an average father, walking slowly,
   To circumvent it in an afternoon,
And any healthy mother to halloo the children
   Back to her . . . from their games across:
Anything bigger than that . . . is an 'estranging sea.'

W. H. Auden, "Lakes"

The question of scale is extremely crucial today, in political, social and economic affairs, just as in almost everything else.

E. F. Schumacher, Small Is Beautiful

Preface

This book is written at a time of disillusionment. Great skepticism has come to surround government programs aimed at the attainment of major social goals. Recent Proposition 13 style tax revolts are but the latest manifestation of a broadly guaged disaffection. The heady optimism of the early 1960s has given way to major doubts concerning the role of government in coping with conspicuous human problems; indeed, among many citizens the conviction has arisen that "government itself *is* the problem."[1]

Perhaps nowhere is this disillusionment more deep-seated than over government projects involving large-scale commitments of public energy and resources. The "war on poverty," welfare, urban renewal, low-income housing and even space and weapons development policies have all come under increasingly critical attack as hopeless boondoggles and extravagant monuments to bureaucratic inefficiency. The belief abounds that largeness-of-scale is itself a major negative element associated with these

[1]Lowi, Theodore J., *The End of Liberalism* (New York: Norton, 1969) p. xiii.

policies—robbing them of the imagination, flexibility and responsiveness they require for success.

Yet it appears that, for good or evil, largeness-of-scale has become one of the most distinctive features of modern governmental organization, just as it has come to characterize society itself. The number and variety of immense public organizations have grown dramatically in the modern era. In addition, the *policies* of these organizations have enlarged as well—involving more citizens, higher costs and more elaborate public objectives and societal aspirations.

At the same time, we do not truly understand what largeness-of-scale implies in relation to government and its policies. What defines a "large-scale" government undertaking, and in what ways is it distinguishable from smaller ones? While many decry the "bigness" of government, we hardly begin to comprehend the consequences of scale—the ways in which it actually affects organizational and interpersonal processes.

This book is directed to this gap in understanding. Specifically, it is designed to investigate the question: To what extent does largeness-of-scale make a qualitative difference in the conduct of public policy?

It is essential in undertaking this task to begin by devoting attention to the concept of scale itself: what it has been assumed to mean and what it should mean in the policy context. Understanding the concept of scale is, as we shall see, no easy assignment. The literature of organization theory, for instance, is littered with the charred remains of numerous attempts to define "size" and to relate size to other organizational properties. This literature is as confusing as it is inconclusive. If it teaches us anything, it is that we must avoid overly narrow definitions of scale that index essentially trivial properties. Moreover, there is a relativity implicit in the concept of scale upon which many analytical efforts can founder. How large does an organization, or policy, have to be before it can appropriately be classified as large in scale?

For our purposes scale will apply not to a single narrow variable but to the relationship between multiple properties. Scale implies a notion of *proportion*—the relationship between plural characteristics as those characteristics are subject to enlargement or contraction. This study will attempt to identify a distinctive class of large-scale policy enterprises—enterprises distinguishable on the basis of an unusual proportionate relationship that obtains among their constituent parts. This relationship among policy components or requisites is not reproducible at shifting values for these components, thus rendering large-scale policies "scale-specific" with respect to their behavior and essential character.

Once large-scale policies are identified, we shall see that a number of secondary characteristics stem from their scale- specificity. Many of these traits raise dramatic challenges to both the analysis of public policy making and the practice of public administration.

In explicating the phenomenon of large-scale policy, a comparative analysis will be undertaken of three major public pursuits—each of which has involved high aspirations and each of which has been subject to widespread public attention. These policies are manned space exploration, the "war on poverty" and the "war on cancer." Only one, manned space exploration, is archetypically large-scale in our terms. Its analysis, supplemented by additional examples, will explain the defining traits of scale and illustrate their political and administrative consequences.

The war on poverty and war on cancer illustrate variations on the central theme. They illustrate the ways in which critical scale mismatches can occur between the structural requirements of a policy enterprise and the political environment within which it is forced to operate. These mismatches can take the form of large-scale policy designs encased in restrictive surroundings or essentially small-scale pursuits greatly amplified by expansive and growth-inducing environments. In either case, the proportionate relationship necessary among policy requisites for politically acceptable performance is not obtained.

This study is designed neither to justify nor attack large-scale undertakings, but rather to identify for analysis important characteristics associated with their pursuit. Ultimately, an understandng of these characteristics may allow for more enlightened policy decisions regarding large-scale objectives—decisions that weigh their political costs with potential benefits. At the same time, it is hoped that the theory of scale presented here, beyond its own ultility or weaknesses, will focus attention on the potential explanatory importance of scale to the understanding of perhaps a wide variety of political processes.

Acknowledgments

This study could not have been written without the cooperation and support of a variety of people at many institutions. At the National Aeronautics and Space Administration, Dr. Eugene Emme, NASA Historian, was particularly helpful in orienting the author to the agency and its extensive in-house literature. Thomas Anderson (also of the Historical Office), Jay Holmes and Thomas Ray (both of the Office of Manned Space Flight) gave their time generously and greatly aided the research. I would also like to thank the NASA library staff for the free rein they allowed me in the use of their resources.

At the then Office of Science and Technology, Dr. Harold Glazer displayed great knowledge of both space exploration and the problems of scale. Dr. Carl York was also very helpful. K. Guild Nichols, staff consultant to the House Committee on Science and Aeronautics, offered a number of insights into legislative impacts on the space program.

At the National Science Foundation, during a summer's employment, a number of persons were of great assistance, among them Raymond Bisplinghoff, Deputy Director (and a former Deputy Administrator of NASA), Richard Green, Wayne Gruner and David Ryer.

|xvi| At the Johns Hopkins University, Matthew Crenson offered many important observations and much useful advice. Nicholas Leggett engaged the author in many lively space-related discussions.

At the University of Tennessee, Joseph Dodd, Anne Hopkins and T. Alexander Smith read much of the manuscript and were instructive and supportive colleagues. Todd LaPorte of the University of California at Berkeley offered many perceptive criticisms that have immeasurably advanced the work. At Elsevier, William Gum provided very constructive editorial aid—with great patience.

Finally, no one at any institution was more important to this study than Francis E. Rourke of Johns Hopkins. His insights, advice and expressions of encouragement are major personal resources upon which this author has come very gratefully to rely. This is a debt for which no thanks can ever be "large" enough.

Introduction:
Policy Paradigms and the Theory of Scale

1

There is an intriguing theme frequently found in works of science fiction, in horror movies, in children's books and occasionally in social satire. It is the idea of giantism: the notion that human beings or other organisms can somehow attain enormous size relative to their environments—well beyond the norm for their species. Such expansion in size is generally accompanied by death, destruction and widespread terror as the giant organism is unable to coexist with a social order of conventional proportions. There is much significance to this theme, for it suggests simultaneously both the importance and complexity of the concept of *scale.*

Perhaps no physical characteristics can as conclusively condition an organism's relationship to its environment as those pertaining to scale. The scale of an organism can directly affect its environmental demands and at the same time condition its response and defense capacities. The relative scale of environmental objects can, in turn, affect the behavior of the organism by triggering or eluding its attention, signaling danger or suggesting vulnerability.

Man, as an organism, can be behaviorally conditioned by factors of scale. The scale of man's geographical surroundings can influence the development of government and culture.[1] Scale in human architecture can convey widely differing impressions of importance, grandeur or intimacy. Human size variations can, in themselves, affect life opportunities or impart distinctive psychological outlooks to persons at species extremes.

Given this importance, it is not surprising that the concept of scale has been the subject of widespread (if sporadic) attention within a variety of research disciplines. In biology, for example, it has long been understood that scale affects the metabolic rates of organisms, and that the consequences of enlarging scale can limit their growth.[2]

In economics, the concept of scale has also had an impact. Economies and diseconomies of scale are considered important factors in the analysis of major industrial processes and their organization.[3] Also in historical analysis, scale has been the subject of attention. Historian Karl Wittfogel has argued that large-scale irrigation projects were closely associated with the development of oriental despotism. Wittfogel perceives an important distinction between "a farming economy that involves small-scale irrigation (hydro-agriculture) and one that involves large-scale and government-managed works of irrigation and flood control (hydraulic agriculture)."[4]

In spite of these applications, however, scale remains a profoundly difficult and troubling concept. What exactly do we mean when we speak of largeness or smallness of scale? Frequently we allude simply to the external, physical dimensions of an object or organism. But scale implies much more than this. Let us consider the theme of giantism again, by way of illustration.

Many fiction connoisseurs are fascinated by this theme because it appears to possess an intriguing plausibility. On the surface it seems distinctly possible that a living system that exists at one scale could find expression at many others. But scale is a quality deep in causal

[1]For discussion of these scale influences, see such works as Barker, Ernest, *The Politics of Aristotle* (Oxford: Clarendon, 1968) Book VII; Gettys, Warner E., Human ecology and social theory, *Social Forces*, 18 (May, 1940): 469–476; and Thomas Franklin, *The Environmental Basis of Society* (New York: Appleton-Century-Croft, 1925). For a classic discussion of the role of geographical and population scale in the control of political faction, see Madison, James, "Federalist #10" in *The Federalist Papers*, edited by Roy P. Fairfield (Garden City, NY: Doubleday, 1961).

[2]See Telfer, William H. and Kennedy, Donald, *The Biology of Organisms* (New York: Wiley, 1965) p. 203.

[3]See, for example, Townsend, Harry, *Scale, Innovation, Merger and Monopoly* (London: Pergammon, 1968).

[4]Wittfogel, Karl A., *Oriental Despotism* (New Haven: Yale University Press, 1957) p. 3.

texture; it is multifaceted. Scale is, in essence, a concept of *propoi-*
tions, entailing the relationship between *multiple* attributes of objects, organisms or systems. This has enormous implications for a wide variety of disciplinary settings within which scale might be considered and, at the moment, for our theme of giantism.

Any living entity is "a *three-dimensional structure*, and as it increases its linear dimensions its surface area will increase as the square of the linear dimension and its volume as the cube of the dimension."[5] Scale increases, in other words, are defined by diverse *types* of growth within an organism—growth that occurs at *differential rates*. At specific scales, these rates may attain critical imbalances. Volume increases mean rapid gains in overall weight. This weight will be gained at a rate out of proportion to increases in the strength and supporting capacity of an organism's skeletal frame. Thus, unless able to alter qualitatively the physical characteristics of their skeletal material, organisms are sharply limited in the relative scale expansions which they can safely accommodate without being crushed under the burden of their own vastly multiplied weight. This is the prosaic reality behind the literary fantasy of living giants.[6]

At the same time, the theme of giantism illustrates the analytical complexity inherent in the concept of scale. Only when we consider multiple dimensions or attributes of a phenomenon in relation to each other is "scale" likely to be applied successfully to the analysis of that phenomenon. Failure to recognize this complexity of the scale concept has led to many research disappointments in numerous disciplinary areas.

Scale and Social Science Applications

The difficulty of scale applications is well revealed in even the earliest efforts to utilize the concept in social science research. Over two thousand years ago, Aristotle asserted that an ideal population density existed with regard to the city state. According to Aristotle:

> Clearly the best limit for the population of a state is the largest number which suffices for the purposes of life, and can be taken in at a single view.[7]

[5]Telfer and Kennedy, idem. (emphasis added)

[6]For an intriguing explanation of this point see Haldane, J.B.S., "On Being the Right Size," in *The World of Mathematics*, Vol. II, edited by James R. Newman (New York: Simon & Schuster, 1956) pp. 952–957.

[7]McKeon, Richard (ed.), *The Basic Works of Aristotle* (New York: Random House, 1941) p. 1284.

|4| Yet Aristotle was quick to admit that a great deal of confusion surrounded the understanding of "social scale."

> Most persons . . . have no idea what is a large and what is a small state. For they judge the size . . . by the number of its inhabitants; whereas they ought to regard, not their number, but their power.[8]

Two thousand years after Aristotle, scale remains a confused concept in the social sciences. Nowhere in this confusion more evident than in research conducted in the area of organization theory. In sociology, political science and social psychology, intensive energy has been expended in efforts to relate the "size" of an organization to other important organizational variables. This research employs a variety of conceptualizations or indices of size, ranging from number of employees or organization members to organizational output, to the value of resources over which organizational control can be exercised.[9] Studies have been conducted to determine the effects of size (however measured) on worker morale, labor turnover and job performance, and upon the structural features of organizations such as levels of hierarchy and bureaucratization.

Yet for all this research, the findings in regard to size are disappointingly inconclusive. Some studies appear to demonstrate that expansions in size lead to an increase in administrative overhead and to a growth of bureaucracy.[10] Other studies, meanwhile, reveal precisely the opposite.[11] Many analyses indicate that a decline in worker morale is closely associated with increases in organizational size. Yet still others assert that employees bring differing aspirations regarding job satisfaction into large and small organizations *to begin with*.[12]

[8]Ibid., p. 1283.

[9]For the personnel concept of organizational size, see Ingham, Geoffrey K., *Size of Industrial Organization and Worker Behavior* (Cambridge: Cambridge University Press, 1970) and Presthus, Robert, *The Organizational Society* (New York: Vintage Books, 1962). For an organizational output definition, see Revans, R.W., Industrial morale and size of unit, *Political Quarterly* 27 (3) (July/September, 1956): 303−311, and Anderson, Theodore R. and Warkov, Seymour, Organizational size and functional complexity: A study of administration in hospitals, *American Sociological Review* 26 (1) (February, 1961): 23−28. Finally, for a definition of size in terms of organizational resources, see Pugh, D.S., Hickson, D.J., Hinings, C.R., and Turner, C., The context of organization structures, *Administrative Science Quarterly* 14 (1) (March, 1969) pp. 91−114. Another example of indexing size by resources is the annual assessment of the "500 Largest Corporations," compiled by *Fortune* magazine.

[10]See Terrien, W.F., and Mills, D.L., The effects of size upon the internal structure of an organization, *American Sociological Review* 20 (1) (February, 1955): 11−14, and Woodward, Joan, *Industrial Organization* (London: Oxford University Press, 1965).

[11]See Melman, Seymour, The rise of administrative overhead in the manufacturing industries in the United States, 1899−1947, *Oxford Economic Papers* 3 (February, 1961): 62−112; and Blau, Peter M., A formal theory of differentiation in organizations, *American Sociological Review* 35 (2) (April, 1970): 201−218.

[12]Ingham, op. cit., p. 29.

The confusion in organization theory is a good illustration of the difficulties encountered in employing even a limited notion of scale in the social sciences. One organizational analysis even concluded that "size may be rather irrelevant as a factor in determining organizational structure."[13]

But conclusions of this type are seriously misleading. They ignore the potential of a more inclusive concept of scale and the fact that the way this concept is operationalized will determine the research results that follow. No correlation is more reliable than the variables upon which it is based. Simply because organizational "size" has been represented by narrow or conflicting indices leading to inconclusive empirical correlates, there is no reason to assume that a similar fate awaits the more expansive variable "scale."

Here we are back to the complexity of the scale concept. Distinctions have been sought between "large" and "small" organizations without the existence of persuasive ideas as to what we should *mean* by those terms. The narrowness of the variables employed in research on organizational size clearly illustrates a failure to recognize the inclusiveness of scale. Scale, again, entails specific dimensions of size, but it implies additionally a consideration of proportions—the relationship between multiple dimensions of an entity as its size increases. It thus seems reasonable to assume that a "large" organization is distinguishable on the basis of more than one structural feature. Restricting an understanding of scale to structural features alone needlessly reduces its utility. Perhaps such variables as the scope of an organization's goals and the nature of its objectives should also be included in an index of scale. The point is that only at a more inclusive level of analysis are distinctions of "large" and "small" likely to be meaningful and significant correlates revealed.

The successful application of the concept of scale to organization theory and throughout the social sciences awaits this type of theoretical refinement. It may not come easily, but the analytical returns from a well-developed notion of scale could be considerable. It is in this decidedly hopeful spirit that this study of large-scale policy enterprises is undertaken.

Toward a Theory of Policy Scale

The intention underlying this analysis is to offer a theory of largeness-of-scale in connection with the policy-making process. Among other things, the theory asserts that largeness-of-scale im-

---

[13]Hall, Richard B., Haas, J. Eugene, and Johnson, Norman J., Organizational size, complexity and formalization, *American Sociological Review* 32 (6) (December, 1967): 912.

plies distinctive *qualitative* properties insofar as policy making is concerned. It is useful to recall for a moment the model of the giant organism. Should such an organism exist, it will be remembered, the "laws of scale" would require that it be composed of qualitatively different structural material than its more diminutive counterparts. In the same way, we will argue that a class of large-scale policy enterprises exists with very different characteristics from more conventional policy undertakings of smaller scale. The properties of policies in this class, in fact, diverge sharply from the patterns that the dominant theoretical outlooks of policy analysis and political science would lead us to expect.

Our most immediate task is to outline some definitional criteria by which the constituents of this class of large-scale policies may be identified. What, in effect, shall we mean by large-scale public policy? Given the implicit connection of scale and the notion of quantity, it is tempting to index the scale of a public policy undertaking by focusing on those features most readily observable and most easily measurable—such variables, for example, as the number of personnel associated with the undertaking (or affected by it), the total resources committed to the policy (expressible in dollar equivalents), and the number of organizations or institutions involved in the design or delivery of policy outputs all present themselves for consideration as defining features of large-scale policy undertakings. Indeed, intuitively we conjure up one or more of these traits when we think of the large-scale enterprise.

Consider manned space exploration policy by way of illustration. Space exploration programs at their peak involved over 409,000 persons employed in both the public and private sectors. Exploration has also utilized enormous quantities of diverse resources. Fiscal appropriations from 1961 to 1978 totaled over $60 billion. In addition, major amounts of land were utilized (over 114,000 acres in the Atlantic Missile Range area alone) and important research and testing facilities were constructed. Finally, space policy has engendered a staggering number of interorganizational contacts in its pursuit. These have taken the form of interagency programs, grants and contracts, research conferences, hearings, land purchase negotiations and even international treaties governing the installation and administration of tracking and data acquisition stations.

These are impressive characteristics and space exploration is surely a large-scale policy; yet for important reasons *we will not use these variables as defining factors of scale.* They will be treated, instead, as frequent *consequences* or correlates of largeness-of-scale, but with scale itself defined in a different and qualitatively distinctive way. It is important to explain why this will be the case.

Deficiencies in Scale Indices. First, the quantitative indices are, in themselves, inconclusive. How many persons or organizations, or what resource amounts, define a policy as large-scale? The indices offer no way to surmount this problem of indeterminacy because they are only relative in application.

The variables are also difficult to integrate additively into a composite scale index. How are numbers of persons, for instance, to be added to dollars expended or to the number of organizations involved in policy outputs? It is certainly conceivable that a policy undertaking "large" in resource demand could be low in manpower requirements, or that one which is labor intensive might be low in interorganizational involvements. Which variable, then, becomes the *defining* trait for largeness of scale?

There is also a third difficulty with these scale variables—by far the most crucial. They convey nothing of the *goal* attached to a policy enterprise. It seems reasonable to expect that large-scale policies, when defined, should involve large-scale *aspirations* as well as simply enlarged organization features.

Without consideration of what a policy organization is attempting to accomplish—that is, its goal characteristics—the determination of scale seems incomplete and uncertain. Significantly, large-scale organization may not be synonymous with large-scale policy. It is toward policy objectives and their qualities that we turn in the quest for a definition of largeness-of-scale. We do so out of the conviction that a qualitative context is necessary to define appropriately largeness-of-scale.

Scale and Policy Objectives. Consider in general the public policy process. Basically a process of bargaining and adjustment, it is characterized by fluid objectives supported by shifting political coalitions.[14] Public policy goods are apportioned piecemeal—in line with prevailing distributions of power or publicized need. Conventional public policy is transacted in this manner largely because conventional policy objectives are, in essence, highly *divisible*—that is, they may be easily disaggregated *while still maintaining coherent form.* Divisible outputs, in other words, may be readily enlarged or contracted, differentially apportioned among specialized

[14]Such, at least, is the prevailing description of policy dominant in the literature of political science. See, for instance, Truman, David B., *The Governmental Process* (New York: Alfred A. Knopf, 1951); Dahl, Robert A., *Pluralist Democracy in the United States* (Chicago: Rand McNally, 1967); and Lindblom, Charles E., *The Intelligence of Democracy* (New York: The Free Press, 1965). For a more critical assessment of the same phenomenon, see Lowi, Theodore J., *The End of Liberalism* (New York: W.W. Norton and Company, 1969).

|8| constituencies.[15] Let us take tariff policy making, for example. Import tariffs are traditionally highly divisible policy undertakings. Tariffs have been selectively applied and frequently modified, and have dispensed differential benefits to specialized interests in line with the lobbying power of those interests.[16] Countless other public policies in such diverse areas as education, agriculture, housing, law enforcement, land development and medical research all display these identical characteristics. Even regulatory policies, despite symbolic overtures to a "public interest," are cast in highly divisible frameworks of benefit and application.[17]

Conventional policy objectives and payoffs are related in a relatively direct and discernible way to the resources and commitments applied to them. The graph in Figure 1-1 depicts this relationship.

Conceding the difficulty of measuring political resources and indexing policy payoffs, the meaning behind the graph is this: the relation of benefits to costs, under conventional policy, is essentially linear and the proportion by which they relate is readily definable. In most policy cases, resources flow more or less directly to politically articulated interests—such payoffs taking the form of direct payments, subsidies, a variety of governmental services, or simply the public employment of persons as an end in itself. In some instances, administrative costs or overhead may intervene substantially between policy resources and their payoffs. In other instances, it is conceivable that policy payoffs may actually *exceed* resource inputs. This is so because *symbolic* benefits and reassurances might be derived by recipients in ways unrelated to tangible governmental costs.[18] These are limiting cases and, in both, policy resources and payoffs still relate in proportionate and readily discernible ways *through a wide continuum of values* for each.

The divisibility of conventional public policy objectives is well

[15]For a description of this divisibility characteristic in connection with a typology of public policy, see Lowi, Theodore J., American business, public policy, case studies and political theory, *World Politics* 16 (July, 1964): 677–715; and Lowi, Four systems of policy, politics and choice, *Public Administration Review* 32 (July/August, 1972): 298–310.

[16]For an insightful look at tariff or import policy making, see Schattschneider, E.E., *Politics, Pressures and the Tariff* (New York: Prentice-Hall, 1935); and, more recently, Bauer, Raymond A., Dexter, Lewis Anthony, and Pool, Ithiel de Sola, *American Business and Public Policy: The Politics of Foreign Trade* (New York: Atherton Press, 1963).

[17]For an analysis of the extent to which regulatory agencies are subject to capture within the framework of divisible and specialized payoffs, see Fainsod, Merle, "Reflections of the Nature of the Regulatory Process," *Public Policy*, Vol. I (Cambridge: Harvard University Press, 1940); Bernstein, Marvin, *Regulating Business by Independent Commission* (Princeton: Princeton University Press, 1955) and Edelman, Murray, Symbols and political quiescence, *American Political Science Review* 54 (3) (September, 1960): 695–704.

[18]For a treatment of symbolic policy payoffs see Edelman, Symbols and political quiescence, op. cit., and Edelman, *The Symbolic Uses of Politics* (Urbana, IL: University of Illinois Press, 1964).

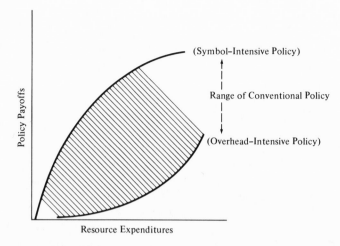

Figure 1-1. Resource payoff relationship: conventional policy.

recognized by both the political analyst and the practitioner. Divisibility assumptions, in fact, underlie the major paradigms that today dominate the discipline of political science. Divisibility, for example, is what lies behind the concept of "pluralism" invariably applied to the analysis of industrialized democracies. Pluralism describes the piecemeal apportionment of public goods in line with prevailing distributions of organized power.[19] Divisibility also supports the common "realist" notion of the public interest as simply the sum total of countless individual interests.[20] Anthony Downs has aptly described this public interest outlook as practiced: "Each decision maker or actor makes whatever choices seem to him to be the most appropriate at that moment, in light of his own interests and his own view of the public welfare."[21]

In addition, the divisibility of conventional public policy objectives is a major underpinning of the incremental model of decision making. Incrementalism, originally described by economist Charles E. Lindblom, is a decision model which asserts the propensity of policy-making organizations to move in small, disaggregated steps.[22] Because of (1) disagreement on primary values and policy

---

[19]See Dahl, op. cit., and Truman, op. cit.

[20]An excellent description of this "realist" approach to the public interest can be found in Schubert, Glendon A., *The Public Interest* (Glencoe, IL: The Free Press, 1961) Chapter 4.

[21]Downs, Anthony, *Urban Problems and Prospects* (Chicago: Markham Publishing Company, 1970): 37.

[22]See Lindblom, Charles E., The 'science' of muddling through, *Public Administration Review* 19 (2) (Spring, 1959): 79–88; and Lindblom and Braybrooke, David, *The Strategy of Decision* (New York: The Free Press, 1963).

objectives and (2) the difficulty of gathering and processing information on which to evaluate a wide range of potential policy options, policy makers typically arrive at their decisions by assessing only "limited comparisons to those policies that differ in relatively small degree from policies presently in effect."[23] The strategy of incrementalism is one of continual policy readjustment in pursuit of marginally redefined policy goals. Long-term plans are abandoned in favor of short-term political implementations. Incrementalism stresses the fluidity and piecemeal nature of the public policy decision process. This and the other major analytical frameworks that dominate political science are dependent on the ability of conventional policies to distribute piecemeal benefits in proportion to varying amounts of political commitment and risk. Under these paradigms, any "large" policy undertaking is simply the accumulation of many small and politically self-contained subprograms and activities.

Now, however, imagine a radically different class of public policy objectives. These objectives entail the provision of *indivisible* payoffs by indivisible means. That is to say, policy benefits cannot be derived in amounts proportionate to resource expenditures. They are, instead, derived in "lumps"—allowing little or no flexibility in their distribution to recipient constituencies.[24] Indivisible payoffs must, in fact, be provided at fixed levels or they simply *cannot be provided at all*.

Economists frequently cite the example of national defense as an indivisible or "collective" public good. But, economists have failed to explore adequately the full range and policy implications of such goods.[25] In addition, the policy objectives in which we are interested are characterized by indivisibilities on the *input* side of the policy equation as well. They depend on commitments, resources and support that are not attainable in flexible quantities.

The Structure of Public Policy

Here a brief discussion of what we might term policy "mechanics" is in order. Without stretching analogies too far it seems safe to say that public policies, like organisms, consist of structural compo-

---

[23]Lindblom, The 'science' of muddling through, op. cit., p. 84.

[24]For a discussion of "lumpy" public goods and their challenge to piecemeal policy-making strategies, see Rose, Richard, Models of governing, *Comparative Politics* 5 (4) (July, 1973): 465–496.

[25]For an interesting application of economic classification schemes to analysis of public policy goods, see Ostrom, Elinor, "On the Variety of Potential Public Goods," unpublished manuscript, Indiana University, 1971.

nents. We might identify some of these as enabling legislation, |11|
budgetary appropriations, personnel, organizational jurisdiction, as
well as some measure of clientele activation and support. Without
the presence of these factors political goals and objectives "float"
ethereally about in the political system—without benefit of policy
support.

In many public policy areas these policy components are available
in a variety of quantities, permitting their flexible combination in
pursuit of specified policy objectives. Appropriations, personnel and
the like can be fitted together at shifting quantities to affect the
amount or intensity of public policy outputs. This variation can be
accomplished without changing the basic qualitative nature of those
outputs.

Large-scale policy enterprises, however, are beset by rigidities in
the availability and combinational flexibility of those policy components necessary for their pursuit. This is so for a number of important reasons which will be explained and illustrated. For these undertakings policy-making requisites are decidedly "lumpy" in their
characteristics of availability and supply. Appropriations and personnel, as we shall see, may be available in very small or quite
substantial quantities, but may not be obtainable in intermediate
quantities. In addition, clientele activation and political support for
pursuit of these policies may be difficult to obtain between the
extremes of apathy and quiescence on the one hand and intensive
arousal on the other.

When one or more of these policy components are available in
inflexible amounts, the combination of all components in a policy
pursuit proves extremely difficult. Clientele activation relative to a
given problem area, for example, may be possible only at high levels
of intensity. Such intensity may demand high levels of appropriation and personnel if it is not to collapse into disillusionment. Such
was the case as we shall see in the war on poverty. Organizational
jurisdiction may also be characterized by inflexibilities in its availability and enlargement. It is often found, for example, that creating
an entirely new public agency can be decidedly easier than marginally extending the jurisdictional coverage of an existing one.[26]
Jurisdictional extensions, if limited in possibility to major enlarge-
ments, may demand high levels of clientele activation or political
support.

Matching policy components with one another when one or more
are characterized by indivisibilities in supply is thus a major chal-

[26]For a discussion of this phenomenon, see Caiden, Gerald E., *Administrative Reform*
(Chicago: Aldine, 1969).

lenge. In some problem areas, combinations of policy factors must be struck by locating what is in effect the "lowest common denominator" among them. This may require the multiplication of some factors to match appropriately others available in indivisible amounts.

Here we are back with the issue of proportions implicit in the concept of scale. For large-scale policy undertakings, the range of relationships that are politically and organizationally feasible among policy components is sharply limited. The combinational possibilities are restricted to distinctive quantities for these components. Just as in the case of an organism, the proportionate relationship necessary among structural components is not reproducible at widely shifting values for these features. For the organism, enlarging its overall dimensions altered the proportionate relationship of its components in untenable ways. For large-scale policy, politically feasible relationships among component parts obtain *only* at high values for these components. If the organism is unreproducible at larger scales, the large-scale policy undertaking cannot find expression at *smaller* scales—that is, at reduced values for its component parts. Large-scale policy, in other words, is *scale-specific* to large and inflexible quantities for its component parts. Politically feasible combinations of policy factors are not derivable from smaller quantities of these components.

It is in this distinctive sense that we will attempt to analyze a class of policy objectives with sharply different characteristics from those outlined in the dominant paradigms of political science and policy analysis. These are policy objectives whose pursuit requires comprehensive rather than incremental commitments and decisions. They require wide-ranging rather than piecemeal resource applications. These are the policies that we will define as large-scale undertakings.

The Large-Scale Public Policy

To review briefly the path taken in defining large-scale public policy: first was a recognition of the difficulties associated with the development of purely quantitative indices of scale. To avoid the inconsistency and indeterminacy of these indices, a more qualitative notion of scale was introduced—namely, scale as the *proportionate* relationship among the components of an entity as a function of its overall dimensions.

In a number of disciplines the concept of scale has assumed such connotations. In architecture, for example, scale implies psycholog-

ical perceptions related to characteristics of proportion. Scale, in |13|
this context, defines a certain "wholeness" about a physical structure.[27]

In much the same way, large-scale public policy can be defined.
This definition asserts the existence of a class of policy objectives
characterized by a distinctive "wholeness" or indivisibility in the
resources or outputs required for their pursuit. Recall the graphic
display by which conventional policies were illustrated. The large-
scale objectives that we are describing look very different, something like what is shown in Figure 1-2.

Here the relationship between policy requisites and policy payoffs
is indirect and discontinuous. Instead of steadily increasing benefits,
the payoff curve defines a *step function*. Intermediate amounts of
policy resources may not be available, and even if available, do not
necessarily yield proportionate gains in policy output; indeed, they
may yield no appreciable or politically sustainable outputs at all.
Yet at a given resource level, the gains derived in policy performance
increase substantially. This reflects the onset of new combinational
possibilities among policy components and their translation into
enhanced payoffs, i.e., the indivisibility connected with largeness-
of-scale. A large-scale policy pursuit thus possesses, as will be demonstrated, special properties that are not duplicated by the simple
accretion of many smaller undertakings.

Indivisibility in large-scale policy, we might say, takes the form of
thresholds—discrete transitions in the availability of policy requisites and in their combinational possibilities—that define a set of
qualitatively different performance patterns.[28] It is the existence of
such thresholds that lies at the heart of largeness-of-scale. They
distinguish large-scale from conventional policy objectives. I em-
phasize that the existence of thresholds is only quite imprecisely
reflected in those organizational factors (appropriations, personnel,
etc.) actually associated with ongoing policy efforts. It is not the
actual *amount* of resources committed to a policy venture that defines it as large-scale. It is their overall characteristics of *availability
and supply* that make the difference. It is distinctly possible, in
other words, for a large-scale administrative and organizational
framework to surround an essentially small-scale and divisible pol-

[27]See Licklider, Heath, *Architectural Scale* (New York: George Braziller, 1965) esp. Chapters 3,
4 and 5.

[28]For an interesting treatment of the analytical problems posed by thresholds, see Simon,
Herbert A., "Some Strategic Considerations in the Construction of Social Science Models," in
Mathematical Thinking in the Social Sciences, edited by Paul Lazarsfeld (Glencoe, IL: The Free
Press, 1954) esp. pp. 402–407.

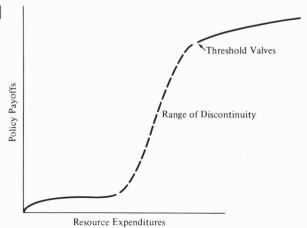

Figure 1-2. Resource payoff relationship: large-scale policy.

icy objective. These circumstances are very different, as we will see, from the special class of large-scale policies to which we have been referring.

The Sources of Policy Indivisibility

It is one thing to postulate a quality of indivisibility connected with a class of public policies; it is quite another to demonstrate this quality plausibly. If, as has been said, the measure of resources actually committed to an ongoing policy effort is not a reliable indicator of its largeness-of-scale, how are we to make this identification? If indivisibility manifests itself in thresholds related to policy requisites and performance, how are such thresholds to be recognized? Does recognition, of necessity, come after the fact, after a policy performance record has been established? How can policy performance, moreover, be traced conclusively to thresholds, as opposed to the vagaries of chance occurrences, political intrusions or bureaucratic inefficiencies? What we must do to deal with these questions is to locate, as precisely as possible, the sources of indivisibility in large-scale objectives.

In essence, the indivisibility that we seek to uncover resides in the *nature of the problem* addressed by policy objectives. Policy endeavors are preceded by definitions of issues or problems for which public action is deemed appropriate. This process of problem definition, in fact, may prove to be the most crucial stage in all political action. (It remains a process largely untreated in policy theory at present.) Policy problems, once defined, display distinctive sets of technical, psychological and political characteristics. Special technical demands, for example, may be imposed on policy efforts by the nature of the problem addressed. Technical "states of the art" may limit alternative routes to the attainment of a given solution or end.

In the same sense, a defined policy problem may impose distinctive psychological conditions or requirements on policy undertakings. A special "turn-of-mind" might need to be overcome, or purposefully imposed, in order to mount an attack on a given problem. Public health policy in developing nations, for instance, has had to overcome many superstitions regarding the sources and inevitability of infectious disease.

A host of specialized political factors also attend specific policy problems. The nature of the defined problem can be a primary influence in the arousal of political interest and support. It can affect the ease with which coalitions can be formed or maintained. Each problem area, in other words, has its own limits to political *feasibility*—limits which impose themselves on policy options.

Finally, indivisibility can derive from the logic of a specific policy *design* which, for whatever reason and with whatever justification, has been selected and applied to the resolution of a public problem. Here it is the policy design itself, once chosen, which can impose distinctive action requirements.

Isolating these dimensions of policy *problems* as sources of indivisibility directs attention to the *content* of public policy; that is, to the nature of what is being done. It is important to recognize the distinctiveness of this focus.

Conventional analysis of the policy process all too often defines policy solely in terms of the political and organizational behavior involved in its pursuit—quite apart from the nature of the goals toward which that behavior is directed. It is only relatively recently, in fact, that some policy analysts have come to question this narrow "form-oriented" approach.[29] There are a growing number of analysts who have come to feel that qualities of content—the intrinsic nature of what is being done—also define "policy" and that characteristics of this content can influence political and organizational behavior in important ways.[30]

It is within this emerging school that our analysis of the sources

[29]For a variety of challenges to conventional policy analytic approaches, see Ranney, Austin (ed.), *Political Science and Public Policy* (Chicago: Markham, 1968).

[30]See, in particular, Froman, Lewis Jr., "The Categorization of Policy Content," in Ranney, op. cit., pp. 41–52, and Salisbury, Robert H., "The Analysis of Public Policy: A Search for Theory and Roles," in Ranney, op. cit., pp. 151–175.

of policy indivisibility firmly resides. Large-scale policy is defined by the existence of objectives that require, in their pursuit, the breach of important thresholds. These thresholds generally arise within those specific dimensions to policy problems mentioned earlier: (1) technology, (2) psychological receptivity, and (3) political mobilization and support. It is time to explore them now in more detail.

Fulfillment of Technical Requisites. Every policy problem poses some sort of technological challenge. The technology requirements associated with its attack or resolution may range from extremely indirect ones (such as computerized accounting or management information systems) to the development of complex hardware (as in spaceflight or weapons policy). Quite frequently a policy problem will yield ground to a variety of different technological tacks, or, at least, plausible arguments can be made for different technological approaches. In the case of large-scale policy pursuits, however, the causal character of the problem, combined with technical states of the art, foreclose all but a few technological options. Further, large-scale policy objectives often require the deployment of complex technologies of a rather rigid and demanding character.[31] Stephen Zwerling, in this regard, has very usefully distinguished "prescriptive" from "adaptive" technologies.[32] A prescriptive technology, such as a nuclear power plant, supersonic transport or railed rapid transit system, requires high sunk costs and comprehensive planning, and is justified only by a "specific vision of the future." This is in contrast to an adaptive technology, such as a bus system, which can be incrementally developed, flexible in design and application, and which "serves the present and is believed to be capable of meeting future needs as well provided that the future is not drastically different from the past."[33]

In effect, a prescriptive technology presents a "quantum" case in which technological capacities are not derivable in piecemeal packages. Even minimal technical performance demands the full-scale development of a comprehensive technological system. In their reliance upon prescriptive technologies, indivisibility is imposed upon large-scale policy undertakings.

[31]For a discussion of the implications of complexity for the development and control of systems, see LaPorte, Todd R., (ed.), *Organized Social Complexity: Challenge to Politics and Policy* (Princeton: Princeton University Press, 1975) esp. Chapters 1, 4, 8 and 10.

[32]Zwerling, Stephen, *Mass Transit and the Politics of Technology: A Study of BART and the San Francisco Bay Area* (New York: Praeger Publishers, 1975).

[33]Zwerling, op. cit., pp. 12−15.

Demand for Specialized Psychologies. Another set of unusual requirements associated with large-scale policy objectives are psychological in nature. Specific "psychologies-of-task" are frequently demanded because of the expansive and risk-taking character of the objective. In the early days of space research, doubts about the time frame and, indeed, the feasibility of manned flight were commonplace, even among recognized aeronautical "authorities." Yet technological and organizational advances in this area required heightened aspirations and intensified confidence approaching that of the classic "revolution of rising expectations." Without such expansive psychologies it would have been difficult to develop an institutional climate conducive to innovation and risk taking.[34] At the same time, NASA officials made repeated efforts to promote an intensive emotional commitment and personal identification with the space program among its contractors and their employees. This was done in recognition of the need to foster great care in the construction of equipment, given the extremely close quality control tolerances demanded by spaceflight hardware.

Compatible psychologies are demanded not only of internal participants in a large-scale policy, but equally from clients and the public as well. Expanded public expectations are essential to stimulate the high intensity resources and political commitments which large-scale objectives are likely to require. In the war on poverty, for example, it was the novel belief in the possibility of actually eradicating poverty (historically a rather heady optimism indeed) that first attracted President Kennedy to the idea of an antipoverty program. This belief was transformed into a national mandate by President Johnson, leading ultimately to the passage of the Economic Opportunity Act of 1964.[35] At the same time, the heightened aspiration of lower income citizens themselves was a major factor in increasing their political activity and organizational participation on behalf of the poverty program.

The Mobilization of Support. An additional source of indivisibility in large-scale policy is the need for broad and continuing political support. The large amounts of economic and social resources required by these policies for their pursuit can only be provided, in highly pluralist and competitive settings, if there is unusually

---

[34]See, for example, Argyris, Chris, *Organization and Innovation* (Homewood, IL: Irwin, 1965) for a discussion of how innovative output varies as a function of organizational culture.

[35]For an interesting description of the evolution of antipoverty perspectives in the White House, see Sundquist, James L., "Origins of the War on Poverty," in *On Fighting Poverty,* edited by Sundquist (New York: Basic Books, 1969) pp. 6–33.

wide-ranging and intensive political support. Such support will generally have to cut across a number of specialized interests and therefore must be constructed around a national interest or collective purpose theme. The lunar landing goal, with its implied assertion of United States space competition with the Soviet Union, was just such a theme and it succeeded in mobilizing that public and Congressional support required for manned space exploration policy.

But political support for a large-scale undertaking must not only be extensive, it must have the prospect of continuity over the long run. It was the long-term nature of the Kennedy commitment to space exploration that made elaborate and expensive start-up efforts seem worthwhile. Technical manpower training and recruitment success closely depended upon the perception of a bright future for the space program.

In generating support along the dimensions they require, large-scale policies are frequently "sold" to the public in expansive, if not grandiose terms. Space and poverty policy, the interstate highway system and even the war in Vietnam were all portrayed in such terms in order to overcome the political support thresholds associated with their pursuit. As we will see, this is a strategy which is not without its hazards.

Policy Indivisibility and Political Analysis

Here, then, are three major requisites attached to the pursuit of a special set of policy objectives. They are requisites that impart an indivisibility to an unusual class of public undertakings—"large-scale" undertakings in our vernacular. This is an important class of public policies. While small in number, the members of this class have vastly magnified consequences. They involve large numbers of citizens and command major shares of the public budget. They are generally directed toward the alleviation of major social problems, the development of new technologies or the attainment of collectivized aspirations. Frequently, large-scale policies have intensive and diverse ramifications throughout the political system—spawning unintended second- and third-order consequences. And, again, this is a class of policies which eludes much of the analytical weaponry of conventional policy research.[36]

Caught up in divisibility and incremental outlooks, we have gained little insight into the politics surrounding the pursuit of ob-

[36]For a critical examination of the analytical issues posed by many large-scale objectives see Nelson, Richard R., *The Moon and the Ghetto: An Essay on Public Policy Analysis* (New York: Norton, 1977).

jectives of a very different order. We have ignored the significance of |19| large-scale phenomena.

This book is designed to offer an alternative to a dominant point of view. It is designed to explore the traits and implications of large-scale policy. The exploration will be conducted around a major theme with two variations. The major focus will be on manned space exploration. Space policy serves well as an archetypical example of a large-scale public undertaking, in both its defining and secondary characteristics. No better examples of indivisibility can be offered than those connected with the pursuit of space exploration objectives. At the same time, space policy was conducted within a correspondingly large organizational and resource framework. As former NASA administrator James Webb asserted:

> No large effort in which we have yet been engaged began with a more imaginative or complete base of legislative authority. None required such rapid advances in so many disciplines—engineering, physics, astronomy, mathematics, economics, political science, psychology, public administration. . . . None had more widespread support, or was carried out so fully in the public view.[37]

Space exploration illustrates at the same time many important political consequences of the pursuit of large-scale undertakings. As we shall see, large-scale policy entails unusual political and organizational mobilizations in the period of its start-up. Largeness-of-scale also contributes secondarily to the development of two unusual decision "types"—"go/no-go" and reflexive decisions—both of which raise real difficulties insofar as accountability and policy guidance are concerned. In addition, large-scale policy is beset by unusual political instabilities. It is unable to balance itself between internal imperatives pushing for expansion and external entropic forces leading to decay.

But space exploration is almost too archetypical an example to provide a fully realistic picture of the large-scale phenomenon in public policy. It matches too well the indivisibility requirements inherent in policy objectives with the resources and supporting organizational framework actually assembled in pursuit of these objectives. Such closeness-of-fit can rarely be expected in "real world" political processes. As has been stated, large-scale policy objectives do not necessarily imply large-scale funding and organization. Also, enlarged resource and organizational frameworks do not guarantee the pursuit of large-scale policy. Two additional policy explications

---

[37]Webb, James E., *Space-Age Management: The Large-Scale Approach* (New York: McGraw-Hill, 1969) p. x.

will be offered to cover these possibilities: the cases being the war on poverty and the war on cancer.

The war on poverty, of course, has been subject to a multitude of conflicting interpretations and evaluations. From our standpoint, however, the poverty program will be offered as an example of how large-scale policy objectives can reside unsuccessfully within a mismatched resource and organizational setting. Antipoverty objectives (however well or poorly chosen) entailed thresholds that remained unbreached in the inchoate and divisible "distributive politics as usual" setting within which the policy came to be transacted. This, it will be argued, may account for many of the failures associated with antipoverty policy.

The war on cancer will be offered as an example of a mismatch in scale in the opposite direction. Here an essentially small-scale policy objective—decidedly plural and divisible in nature—has been cast on an inappropriately *large* organizational scale. This mismatch, as a growing number in the biomedical research community are asserting, threatens to result in rigidity of outlook, misdirected effort and wasted resources.

A major analytical challenge posed by the theory of scale is to learn to identify mismatches such as these and, in a larger sense, to determine when and whether large-scale pursuits are appropriate. At the same time, the theory of scale has major implications for policy making as presently practiced.

Large-Scale Policy and Pluralist Processes

Large-scale policy objectives, as we will see, are not easily reconciled to the dominant political environment of pluralist bargaining and scarce resources. The danger looms that many important policy objectives will fail to be realized because they will prove to be large-scale objectives for which commitment and resources could not be obtained at requisite levels. Large-scale policies are extremely vulnerable to the compromise and reduction processes of distributive politics.

Yet at the same time it is necessary to protect the divisible policy environment from the dangers implicit in large-scale undertakings. It is bargaining and compromise, after all, that allow diverse interests to coexist. The provision of divisible public goods, reflecting piecemeal social commitments, leads to stability and flexibility in the political system; it allows processes of accountability to be imposed onto policymaking in what is perceived to be a responsive manner. Large-scale policy, with its requirements for high-intensity

political mobilization and relatively inflexible, long-term resource
commitments, (not to mention its self-escalating qualities with respect to both mobilization and resources) threatens to undermine
many important features of pluralist democracy.

These are issues with which we are likely to be increasingly confronted. Many of our societal aspirations regarding energy resources,
transportation and urban redevelopment may well require large-
scale policy approaches. Either we will have to downgrade these
aspirations or establish more congenial political environments
within which large-scale undertakings can operate (while hopefully
safeguarding ourselves from the threatening consequences).

Our first order challenge, however, would seem to be the
heightening of insight regarding the large-scale phenomenon. We
need to learn more about the sources of policy indivisibility, how to
predict the existence and extent of performance thresholds, and
what precisely the set of political characteristics *are* that come to
surround the pursuit of large-scale policies. To do this, we must
begin to construct new analytical frameworks capable of ordering
phenomena which currently elude the coverage of the dominant
paradigms in policy analysis and political science. It is hoped that
this book will be a tentative step in that new direction.

The Start-Up Politics of Large-Scale Policy

On May 25, 1961, President John F. Kennedy, in a special message to Congress, proclaimed the goal of landing a man on the moon and returning him safely to earth. This was to be accomplished before the end of the decade—an undertaking explicitly designated as a major national commitment.

In communicating his intentions to the Congress the President indicated that space-related budget allocations were to be enlarged, and that the pace of spacecraft and booster development was to be accelerated. In the ensuing five fiscal years National Aeronautics and Space Administration appropriations rose from $1.8 billion to $5.2 billion, and total employees associated with space exploration programs (both within and outside of NASA) climbed form less than 60,000 to a peak of 409,000.[1] .

Yet the Kennedy announcement came a full four years after the birth of the "space race"—the launching of the Soviet satellite Sputnik I. What about the nation's space enterprise during this four-year interim period? The answer is signif-

[1]"Statistical Report," *National Aeronautics and Space Administration*, Program and Special Documents Division, (Washington, DC: U.S. Government Printing Office, 1971).

icant and revealing. It illustrates the "start-up" dilemmas associated with large-scale policy objectives.

Public Policy vs Public Pressure

The history of manned space exploration in the interim period between the launch of Sputnik I and the Kennedy commitment is one of opinion intensity in the midst of organizational insufficiency. The Sputnik launch (and its more spectacular sequel, the canine-carrying Sputnik II) had aroused within the United States both a sense of alarm at the technological and projected military capabilities of the Soviet Union, and a mood of exasperation at the slow-moving pace of U.S. missile and rocket development.[2] A U.S. Senator termed the Sputnik launch and its immediate aftermath "a week of shame and disaster."[3] *Life* magazine warned its readers that "the U.S. cannot lag . . . behind Communism; indeed we must recover our lead to strengthen our hand in seeking a reasonable agreement with Russia that free nations can accept."[4] And the *New Republic* asserted that for space exploration, "a completely new spirit is needed if our efforts are to prosper, a spirit of buoyant determination that does not thrive in an economy atmosphere. There must be, in some substantial measure, an actual *reversal* of the tax-and-budget-cut trend of the last few years."[5] Clearly the mood was right for a public policy effort of major proportions.

Yet, set apart from the "buoyant determination" generated by the success of Sputniks I and II stood the inchoate and disordered organizational and administrative network responsible for the development of a United States space exploration capability. At the heart of this administrative apparatus was the National Advisory Committee for Aeronautics (NACA). Small and relatively obscure, NACA served as a research and consultative agency for other divisions of the federal government (particularly the Air Force) and for the aeronautics industry. NACA had established a long history of pioneer research in aeronautics; yet, after Sputnik, it became an agency beset by crisis. It was clear that "unless NACA moved rapidly and adroitly it might very well be overwhelmed in the national clamor for radical departures."[6]

Apart from NACA, each of the three military services conducted

[2]This unfavorable contrast between United States and Soviet space efforts was heightened by the spectacular failure, nationally televised, of a Vanguard test satellite launch—barely two months after the successful launch of Sputnik I.

[3]Jackson, Senator Henry M., as quoted in *Time*, 70(17) (October 21, 1957):21.

[4]Common sense and Sputnik, *Life*, 43(17) (October 21, 1957):35.

[5]*The New Republic*, 137(21) (November 11, 1957):4.

[6]Grimwood, James M., Swenson, Lloyd S. Jr., and Alexander, Charles C., *This New Ocean: A History of Project Mercury* (Washington, DC: U.S. Government Printing Office, 1966) p. 75.

| 24 | piecemeal research and development operations. These operations were directed toward the dimension of astronautics that squared with each service's highly specialized conception of what space exploration was all about. To the Army, astronautics implied ballistic missiles, and such missiles were clearly within the Army purview since they represented logical extensions of ground artillery. The Army Ballistic Missile Agency, staffed by the "von Braun team" of captured German rocket engineers, focused its research attention on fuels, thrusts and payload capacities. The Redstone and Jupiter-C were the Army's primary rocket development projects.

Meanwhile, the Air Force treated space flight as an extension of air flight—a philosophy that placed space research firmly within the aeronautics programming to which it had previously been committed. The Air Force's Air Research and Development Command investigated materials stresses, spacecraft design and the human factors associated with space flight—life support, acceleration and deceleration tolerances, etc.

Finally, the Navy's Bureau of Aeronautics was researching satellite instrumentation and tracking. The Navy was also heavily involved in the development and deployment of high-altitude balloons and sounding rockets, as well as experimentation with human space flight stresses.

During this period a great deal of criticism was directed at these military research and development programs. It was alleged that progress in space was delayed by harmful competition and wasteful overlap.[7] That there was intensive competition among the services for primacy in space exploration can hardly be doubted.

By 1958 the Army was strongly pushing for Defense Department approval of what it termed its "Man-Very-High" project. In formulating its plans, the Army manned space research group "had unearthed one of their old proposals for using a modified Redstone to launch a man in a sealed capsule along a steep, or suborbital, trajectory."[8]

The Air Force, meanwhile, countered the Army's "Man-Very-High" project with one of its own entitled, "Man-In-Space-Soonest." This was to be a four-phased program, beginning with the orbiting of instrument packages and culminating in the launch of a manned capsule late in 1960.[9]

[7]This critical theme pervades much of the Congressional investigation of U.S. space activies during the interim period before the Kennedy lunar landing commitment. See, for example, "Investigation of Governmental Organization for Space Activities," *Hearings Before the Committee on Aeronautical and Space Sciences, United States Senate, 86th Congress, First Session* (Washington, DC: U.S. Government Printing Office, 1959).

[8]Grimwood et al., *This New Ocean*, op. cit. p. 99.

[9]See "Chronology of Early USAF Man-In-Space Activity, 1955 to 1960," *Air Force Systems Command* (Washington, DC: U.S. Government Printing Office, 1961).

Finally, the Navy, not to be outdone, presented its entry in what had by now become a domestic space race, with space in the defense appropriations budget as the most sought after prize. The Navy's proposal was for "Project MER" (Manned Earth Reconnaissance), a highly innovative approach to manned space exploration featuring a spacecraft with its own self-contained gliding capability in order to facilitate recovery.[10]

This interservice competition, though intensive, was not entirely harmful; nor did it always lead to as much overlap and duplication as its critics have suggested. Despite the existence of competing programs, interservice *cooperation* also played a prominent role in the advancement of space technology. The X-15, for example, considered by many aviation specialists to be one of the most successful research projects ever undertaken, was a joint Air Force and Navy enterprise.[11] Moreover, a great deal of informal specialization was practiced by the services as they sought advancements that would heighten the relative attractiveness of their individual research and development programs. The tri-service approach to space research to this extent broadened the available sources of technological innovation—enlarging the base of theory and experimental data from which space policy planners were eventually to draw.

The final major component in the organizational network associated with space exploration in this post-Sputnik "interim" period was American the aerospace industry.

The U.S. aircraft industry, of course, was well developed at the time of Sputniks I and II. It was also actively involved in missile development under contract to a variety of Defense Department weapons procurement programs. Yet the aircraft industry was not primed during this period for extensive participation in manned space exploration. Specific feasibility studies had been undertaken by a few major industries in response to individual service research projects. But these studies were far removed from major development contracts. The von Braun research team of the Army Ballistic Missile Agency had even established "a rocket development center where its own vehicles could be evolved 'in house' rather than by outside contractors."[12] And the Martin Company held its work on the Vanguard Satellite program in such low regard that the engineering group assigned to work on the project was confined to an attic in the company's oldest aircraft plant in Baltimore. As if the extremes of temperature to which this location subjected the engineers were not trauma enough, "the harried staff also had to cope with the

[10]Grimwood et al., op. cit., p. 100.

[11]See Stilwell, Wendall H., *X-15 Research Results* (Washington, DC: U.S. Government Printing Office, 1965).

[12]Lewis, Richard S., *Appointment on the Moon* (New York: Viking Press, 1968) p. 36.

droppings of pigeons which were flitting from rafter to rafter over-head."[13] Obviously, an extensive and coordinated participation by private industry in manned space exploration programs had yet to be established.

This early period in the history of the U.S. space program, where substantial public pressures confronted a disordered policy framework, reveals an important relationship between public policy and public pressure. Public pressure generally oscillates widely within a political system—often enlarging rapidly, then declining suddenly.[14] These oscillations can occur anywhere along a continuum of intensity primarily as a function of complex determinants of attitude and attention.

Yet public policy is not similarly free to move along a continuum insofar as its operating scale is concerned. Much has been said in public administration about the "incremental" nature of policy decisions.[15] Yet relative to public pressure, public policy is beset by a dependence on organizational features which cause it to enlarge or contract in discontinuous "jumps" as jurisdictional, manpower or budgetary plateaus are reached. Figure 2-1 illustrates the point.

Recognizing the enormous uncertainties in the meaning (and consequences) of public pressure, and granting the formidable methodological problems in indexing its expansion, the meaning behind the graph is this: given the highly disparate ways in which policy and pressure enlarge it is *unlikely for them ever to be found appropriately matched.* Pressure expands as a continuous function (although, as mentioned earlier, it is subject to wide and rapid fluctuations along its intensity continuum). However, policy capability enlarges as a step function. It is beset by discontinuities that reflect resistance associated with its expansion. Enabling legislation, for example, is often required for the initiation of a policy pursuit. Once established, a policy is not likely to expand far from the dimensions of its birth without soon confronting jurisdictional, manpower and appropriations boundaries. Then it must *leap* over these boundaries, securing an enlargement of its legislative authorization, upgrading its manpower supplies and justifying an increased level of appropriated funds. This process does not come to define a smooth gradient. It occurs in spurts. Significantly, some policies (including manned

[13]Cox, Donald W., *The Space Race* (New York: Chilton Books, 1962) p. 28.

[14]For an interesting discussion of public opinion "stages" and their determinants see Downs, Anthony, Up and down with ecology—The issue-attention cycle, *The Public Interest* No. 28 (Summer, 1972) pp. 38–50.

[15]See Lindblom, Charles E., The 'science' of muddling through, *Public Administration Review* 19(2) (Spring, 1959): 79–88.

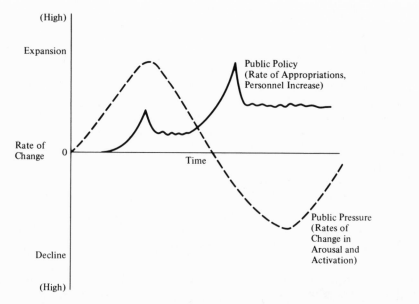

Figure 2-1. Comparative expansion functions: public policy versus public pressure.

space exploration) must expand greatly *if they are to expand at all.* Only then can they overcome the inertia, external resistance or "start-up" factors that act as barriers to policy expansion. It is perhaps a telling illustration of this all too ignored step-function nature of policy enlargement that "the general pattern characterizing the growth of . . . new [Federal] programs is this: sharp increases in the first two years as the programs get into fuller operation, relatively modest increases in the third and fourth years, followed by a steep jump of the sort depicting major expansion or legislative extension of the program."[16]

Let us again look at the policy–pressure relationship illustrated in the graph. As pressure builds for government action in regard to a specific issue, it is likely to confront a vacuum in ongoing public policy. The beginnings of the ecology "movement" amply illustrate this phase, where increased public concern over problems of environmental quality quickly overbalanced the minimal regulatory standards of the Federal government. This initial phase is one of *underscaling* in public policy performance relative to public pressure. Such an underscaling characterized the organizational insuf-

[16]*Growth Trends of New Federal Programs: 1955–1968* (The Tax Foundation, 1967) pp. 19–20.

ficiencies of the space program during the period on which we have so far been concentrating.

Eventually, of course, public policies are generated in response to escalating public pressure. But, again, the discontinuous nature of policy expansion can make it difficult to match appropriately government performance with fluctuations in public "demand." Ultimately, such performance may jump to a level at which it actually *exceeds* public demand. This might well be termed the *overscaling* dimension to public policy. Overscaling too has become an important part of the manned space exploration story. At this extreme of the policy–pressure relationship, bureaucratic practices can persist long after the pressure (and indeed even the interest) for such public pursuits has subsided. This can result in that saddest of administrative spectacles, the politically orphaned agency—an object (in Norton Long's words) "of contempt to its enemies and despair to its friends."[17]

These policy–pressure relationships will play an important role in later aspects of this manned space exploration analysis. At this point, however, they serve to suggest the first fundamental characteristic of the large-scale policy enterprise. *Large-scale policy pursuits are beset by organizational thresholds or "critical mass" points closely associated with both their initiation and subsequent development.* In other words, the large-scale policy enterprise must rely for politically acceptable performance upon a set of factors that come suddenly into play at relatively high levels of political and resource commitment.

The large-scale policy objective typically confronts psychological, technological, organizational and administrative barriers over which it must "leap" discontinuously if it is to establish and sustain itself. It is within this framework that we discuss "start-up" problems in manned space exploration.

Start-Up Thresholds in Space Exploration Policy

We left space exploration in the interim period between the first Soviet Sputniks and the Kennedy moon landing commitment. This was the era of a "lagging, directionless space program"[18] or, as one critic expressed it, a "space maze and missile mess in Washington."[19]

[17]Long, Norton E., Power and administration, *Public Administration Review* 9(4) (Autumn, 1949):257.

[18]Lewis, Richard S., The Kennedy Effect, *Bulletin of the Atomic Scientists* 24(3) (March, 1968):2.

[19]Cox, op. cit., p. 69.

In February of 1958 the Advanced Research Projects Agency (ARPA) was established in the Department of Defense in an attempt to coordinate and oversee the diverse military missile and space satellite programs. This was an initial attempt to upgrade U.S. space exploration in light of conspicuous Soviet successes, yet it proved to be hopelessly underscaled in relation to diverse thresholds that had to be breached and organizational inertias which had to be overcome.

The Dilemma of Thinking Small. The first problem was a psychological one. Perhaps no barrier is more difficult and yet more essential for a large-scale policy enterprise to overcome than the penchant for "thinking small." Overcoming this trait has long been deemed important in developing the receptivity and imagination required to stimulate organizational innovation.[20] Thinking small is also a detriment to the planning and administrative consolidation upon which the large-scale policy enterprise depends.[21]

Before the lunar landing commitment was made, pessimistic estimates of the rate of technological advance possible in connection with manned space exploration were commonplace. Even the highly respected Hugh Dryden, a NACA Director and future Deputy Administrator of NASA, asserted a scant four years before Sputnik: "I am reasonably sure that travel to the moon will not occur in my lifetime. . . ."[22] Such myopia was certainly understandable, yet space policy planning required both foresight and an obstinate faith in the future. It was not until this optimistic perspective was firmly developed that effective preparation for manned missions could begin. One recent analysis, in fact, likens the development of the space program to the spread of a social movement, led by a cadre of scientific "zealots" single-mindedly mobilizing others to acquire their revolutionary zeal.[23]

In the meantime, "thinking small" proved to be a barrier to the jurisdictional expansion that space exploration policy required. NACA, the central research agency in the administrative network concerned with space exploration, actively resisted Eisenhower administration efforts to upgrade its policy jurisdiction. "By February

[20]Argyris, Chris, *Organization and Innovation* (Homewood, IL: Irwin, 1965).

[21]Such has been the case in other large-scale undertakings besides the space program. The need to instill an expansive psychology among policy participants was recognized, for example, in the development of the Polaris weapon system by the Navy. See, on this point, Sapolsky, Harvey, *The Polaris System Development: Bureaucratic and Programmatic Success in Government* (Cambridge: Harvard University Press, 1972) esp. pp. 44–46.

[22]Dryden, Hugh L., as quoted in Grimwood et al., op. cit., p. 56.

[23]Bainbridge, William Sims, *The Spaceflight Revolution: A Sociological Study* (New York: Wiley, 1976).

1958, as the Eisenhower administration began wrestling with the complexities of formulating a national program for space exploration, NACA had taken the official position that with regard to space it neither wanted nor expected more than its historic niche in government-financed science and engineering. While NACA should become a substantially bigger instrument for research, it should remain essentially a producer of data for use by others."[24]

This reluctance to accept an enlarged organizational assignment (and, indeed, to partake in timely jurisdictional growth) led ultimately to the demise of NACA later that same year. In its place the National Aeronautics and Space Act of 1958 established a national space advisory council (The National Aeronautics and Space Council) and the National Aeronautics and Space Administration (NASA), which absorbed most of NACA's personnel. NASA was the agency created to attain the administrative consolidation required for space exploration.

The Necessity for Administrative Consolidation. Even though the Space Act provided for a distinctive civilian/military apportionment of space exploration activity between NASA and DOD, NASA, immediately upon its formation, began to press for the acquisiton of key research groups and programs located within the military services. In less than three months NASA had acquired Project Vanguard from the Navy (as well as the 150 staff members and $25 million in appropriations connected with it), lunar probe and earth satellite projects from the Air Force and the Jet Propulsion Laboratory (complete with Cal Tech staff and $100 million in appropriations) from the Army.[25] It even attempted to take over the Army Ballistic Missile Agency amid cries of outrage from that service. Although delayed by Army opposition, NASA's ambitious plans were not to be denied. In March of 1960 NASA formally acquired the ABMA and most of its key researchers.

These acquisitions reflect the importance to the large-scale enterprise of consolidating control over those suboperations upon which it closely depends. In industrial settings this consolidation occurs as "vertical integration"—a corporate tendency to amalgamate raw materials and component production processes within the same managerial framework as that governing the creation of a final marketable product for which these subprocesses are important.[26] (Of course, at the same time NASA was accomplishing a type of "hori-

[24]Grimwood et al., op. cit., p. 77.

[25]Rosholt, Robert L., *An Administrative History of NASA, 1958–1963* (Washington, DC: U.S. Government Printing Office, 1966) pp. 45–48.

[26]See, for example, Boulding, Kenneth, *Economic Analysis* (New York: Harper, 1955) pp. 501–502.

zontal integration," eliminating sources of space exploration competition.)

The large-scale enterprise requires extensive consolidation because of the close interdependency of its component parts. Uncertainty or performance failures in any one suboperation can threaten the success of them all.[27] Also, many research and development projects require parallel breakthroughs on a variety of problem fronts. The development of a rocket guidance system, for example, necessitated simultaneous advances in both computer miniaturization and thruster engine design.

The Air Force, in early recognition of the need for administrative consolidation in the management of its ballistic missile development, fashioned a complex managerial system which it termed "concurrency." This system involved an intricate reporting and decision network that linked all of the diverse research operations which comprised the Air Force missile development program.[28] A similarly comprehensive managerial edifice was constructed to oversee the development work associated with the Manhattan Project.

For manned space exploration, consolidation was an essential requirement given the extremely large number of development projects on which any manned mission plans would depend. "Whether it was given special responsibilities or not, NASA had to concern itself with the Nation's overall space program *if it was to optimize its own* [emphasis added]."[29]

Administrative consolidation also helped NASA to recruit, both from industry and other government agencies, highly qualified technical personnel to work with its programs. In part, consolidation heightens those public expectations required to mobilize the manpower essential to any large-scale enterprise. As one NASA official observed: "We believe that we are attracting quality people . . . because we have salaries which are competitive, plus a new, attractive and exciting program, and an expanding mission which creates the possibilities of greater opportunities."[30]

[27]This high degree of interdependency is a characteristic closely associated with complex systems in general. As Garry Brewer notes, "The greater the complexity of a system, the less likely is it that it can be decomposed and the more likely that short-run behavior of any one subsystem will ramify throughout the entire system." Brewer, Garry, *Politicians, Bureaucrats and the Consultant* (New York: Basic Books, 1973) pp. 73–74. For further explications of the concept of complexity see LaPorte, Todd R. (ed.), *Organized Social Complexity: Challenge to Politics and Policy* (Princeton: Princeton University Press, 1975).

[28]For a discussion of Air Force missile management see Ritland, O.J., Concurrency, *Air Force Quarterly Review* 12 (Winter/Spring, 1960–1961) pp: 237–250.

[29]Rosholt, op. cit., p. 106.

[30]Silverstein, Abe, Director, Space Flight Programs, NASA in testimony in *Hearings Before the Senate Committee on Aueronautical and Space Sciences, June 7–12, 1961* (Washington, DC: U.S. Government Printing Office, 1961) p. 177.

|32| Related to administrative consolidation were additional start-up barriers that space exploration policy making had to overcome.

The Indivisibility Dimensions of Research. A great deal has been written in the literature on organizational management about the importance and inevitability of specialization both for bureaucratic supervision and institutional problem solving. Yet this attention to specialization has to some extent resulted in neglect of those operations for which specialization is not entirely appropriate. One of these, oddly enough, is the major research project—the very setting in which specialized knowledge would seem most important. But a large-scale research problem is often interdisciplinary, cutting across lines of specialization and imparting an indivisibility to organizational tasks. For these problems "research teams are only divisible down to a minimum effective scale."[31] Conversely, research teams must attain this scale or threshold if they are to attack a critical problem effectively.

A primary reason for the sluggishness in the pace of exploration prior to the Kennedy moon-landing commitment (even after intensive public pressure had mounted for such exploration) was the failure of research and development projects within the military services to reach their "critical mass" points of problem-solving effectiveness. In reality, too much specialization and research diversification precluded those advances that could only occur in interdisciplinary combination. This synergism requirement is closely associated with the general phenomenon of technological change. "It is not uncommon that two or three streams of small-scale innovation coverage and a transition with major consequences results. The results are not merely additive, the combination turns out to be explosive."[32]

One interesting example of an indivisible research problem of the type that permeated space exploration was the design of a contour couch for potential spacecraft passengers. The dimensions to this problem were what are the stresses to which a man is subject in the acceleration and deceleration periods of spaceflight; what factors define human tolerances to these intensified gravitational pressures; and what in the way of structural support could be offered a space traveler given both spacecraft requirements and human limitations?

Arriving at answers to these questions required approximately six

[31]Townsend, Harry, *Scale, Innovation, Merger and Monopoly* (London: Pergamon, 1968) p. 25.

[32]Meier, Richard L., Analysis of the social consequences of scientific discovery, *American Journal of Physics* 25(9) (December, 1957):611. For a more detailed analysis of this "take-off" phenomenon see Schmookler, Jacob, *Invention and Economic Growth* (Cambridge: Harvard University Press, 1966).

years of intensive effort by mathematicians (who assessed probable g-forces during distinct stages of space flight), physiologists (who tested human endurance in a variety of experimental settings) and engineers (who tested a multiplicity of materials and designs in line with experimentally-derived specifications). The final outcome—a fiberglass mold of each astronaut's body contours in a semisupine position—"represented a *combination* of the advantages gained from many experiments by military and other specialists in flight physiology, as well as from the ingenuity of the aeronautical engineers in NACA and NASA."[33]

Research problems of this type delayed progress in space flight technology until interdisciplinary groups could be assembled on a scale that would multiply their problem-solving effectiveness. Below this "critical mass" point a host of conflicting theories and experimental results remained largely unreconciled while still other "good ideas" went begging for attention.

In discussing indivisibilities associated with space exploration research, it is important to note the extent to which much of this research was "equipment-intensive." The study of acceleration tolerances, for example, required the construction of large centrifuges to simulate the stresses of space flight. Research into designs and materials that would safeguard spacecraft reentry into the earth's atmosphere depended upon sophisticated hypersonic wind tunnels, and was delayed pending the construction of such devices.[34]

This "equipment-intensive" characteristic of much of space exploration research heightened its start-up threshold. The design and subsequent construction of specialized instrumentation or simulation devices was expensive, and the scarcity of such equipment served to centralize strains of research activity around a few major groups that had primary access to these devices. These expense and centralization factors that typified space research are not at all unlike the features associated with large-scale science in general.[35] They were responsible for important lags in research progress prior to the policy acceleration which organized and funded research groups at their critical masses of problem-solving effectiveness.

Land Acquisition and Facilities Construction. Another feature of manned space exploration to which start-up thresholds were at-

[33]Grimwood et al., op. cit., p. 46.

[34]See Allen, H. Julien, Hypersonic flight and the reentry problem, *Journal of the Aeronautical Sciences* 25 (April, 1958):217–230.

[35]For a discussion of the organizational features associated with the conduct of large-scale scientific research see Price, Derek J. deSolla, *Little Science, Big Science* (New York: Columbia University Press, 1963) pp. 161–164.

|34| tached was land acquisition and facilities construction. Enormous quantities of land and elaborate spacecraft tracking, construction and testing facilities were required before any manned mission planning could realistically begin.

The Atlantic Missile Range alone covered over 100,000 acres of land. While some of this land had been acquired earlier by the Air Force, far larger tracts were needed by NASA to construct an adequate launch facility. Their acquisition clearly reflected the threshold problems encountered by the large-scale policy enterprise. As it developed, the buying of land was a process not readily susceptible to gradualism. It required both executive branch clearance and specific Congressional authorization—actions which in turn were predicated upon elaborate program justifications. It was not easy to attain these requisites in small measure because of a peculiarity in the approval process. *Program plans had to be large if they were also to be persuasive.* Larger-scale plans communicated a sense of urgency and purpose. In a very real sense, the *scale* of the land acquisition request was a major factor in upgrading the probabilities of its own fulfillment.

A further requisite in the land acquisition process was the need for land holdings to be concentrated at the early stages of agency planning. This was important because the very act of land acquisition (and the publicized prospect of its subsequent development) raised the price (and in some cases altered the zoning) of surrounding land areas in highly unfavorable directions. This made it far more difficult to acquire additional land later. It was for precisely this reason that NASA Administrator James Webb, in requesting Congressional authorization for land acquisition within the Atlantic Missile Range area, argued vigorously for permission "to take all the land that we can visualize that would be required. Once we get this, I do not think it will be possible to get any more land there. It will be too expensive."[36] This peculiar reflexive property of decisions (by which they prove to be either self-fulfilling or self-frustrating) is a major feature of the large-scale policy enterprise. It will be treated in more detail later.

The construction of facilities likewise proved to be a major threshold in the start-up administration of manned space exploration. A global network of tracking stations was required in order to monitor continuously spacecraft in flight. This network required an extensive set of international agreements (negotiated by the State

[36]Webb, James E., testimony on FY 1963 Authorization *Hearings Before the Senate Committee on Aeronautical and Space Sciences* (Washington, DC: U.S. Government Printing Office, 1962) p. 35.

Department) as well as the development and installation of sensi- tive monitoring equipment.[37]

In addition to the tracking stations other major facilities were rapidly constructed. The Goddard Space Flight Center in Greenbelt, Maryland, was established to serve as a relay point between the tracking network and a mission control center. A major launch operations complex was constructed at Cape Canaveral, Florida. A Manned Spacecraft Center was built in Houston to design, develop and test spacecraft for use in manned flights, as well as to recruit and subsequently train the men for those flights. The ABMA operations office in Huntsville, Alabama, was enlarged into the George C. Marshall Spaceflight Center and assigned the responsibility for launch vehicle research and development. Finally, three major booster engine assembly and testing centers were established at White Sands, New Mexico, Michoud, Louisiana, and Bay St. Louis, Mississippi.

It is, of course, true that not all these facilities were critically required for space exploration. One NASA official, when pressed, even admitted "there was an overbuilding of facilities in the early stages of NASA development." Certainly the pork barrel distribution of those facilities (around the "Southern crescent") has not escaped public notice.[38]

Yet many of these facilities were technically required. If there was overbuilding, it reflects the importance attached to the start-up process by space administrators themselves, as well as the rising expectations generally preceding a large-scale endeavor.

The Realization of Economies-of-Scale. A final class of start-up thresholds that characterized space exploration consisted of those operations dependent upon economies-of-scale. The notion of economy-of-scale is a well developed one in the literature of industrial economics. It remains, however, less developed in public administration despite its significance within this area.[39] The realization of economies-of-scale is important to the large-scale public policy enterprise—both because of the need to make the most out of scarcely allocated public funds and because scale can often have a *qualitative* impact upon general policy performance.

[37]For a more detailed analysis of NASA–State Department interactions over tracking installations see Davis, David H., *How the Bureaucracy Makes Foreign Policy: An Exchange Analysis* (Lexington, MA: DC Heath, 1972).

[38]For this "pork barrel" critique as well as a more general attack upon the space program see Etzioni, Amitai, *The Moon Doggle* (New York: Doubleday, 1964).

[39]Perhaps the analysis that comes closest to linking economies of scale with the formation of public policy is that offered by Olson, Mancur, in The principle of fiscal equivalence: The division of responsibilities among different levels of government, *American Economic Review* 59 (May, 1969): 479–487.

Major savings in time, money and manpower resources relative to a given organizational output have often been accomplished as a result of attaining key thresholds of scale. In the United States aircraft industry, for example, an 80 percent economy-of-scale rule has been displayed.

> It was found that every time the cumulative output of an aircraft doubled, the cost of production fell to 80 percent of its previous level. If the cost of producing the 50th aircraft was 100, the cost of producing the 100th would be 80, the cost of the 150th would be 64, and so on.

> The fall in cost is the result of learning from previous production. As the cumulative total of output rises the workforce becomes more experienced and adept, fewer errors are made, improvements in processes are seen and introduced.[40]

Traditionally, cost per unit output has been lessened under the impace of scale increases by means of a variety of specific savings. Set-up costs, for instance, may be simply "once and for all." This means that once any necessary equipment, facility or market has been established, it no longer represents a *repeating* cost as output continues and enlarges. Another economy resides in the fact that, given an increase in the scale of a physical structure, the volume of that structure enlarges at a much greater rate than its surface area. This means that construction costs do not necessarily rise in proportion to increases in storage or housing capacity. Finally, machinery often operates at a "minimum efficient capacity—if overall output is not sufficient to utilize fully this capacity waste can result."[41]

Many of these economies are also prominently utilized in space exploration. Start-up costs, for example, are not repeated as manned missions progress. Many of the R&D undertakings required for these missions had very long lead times and payoffs appropriate only for mission plans projected far into the future. Also, large storage and assembly buildings have cheapened construction costs relative to their general capacity.

In addition to these economies, a number of space exploration requisites are only *qualitatively* realized under the impact of scale. Reliability in space hardware, for instance, a critical dimension to any manned space exploration undertaking, was closely dependent upon a large number of trial tests and subsequent "debugging" after prolonged use. As one NASA official described this problem early in the space program:

> We never quite know, when we launch a satellite, what is going to be the limiting point because we have not been in business long enough

[40]Townsend, op. cit., p. 4.
[41]Ibid., pp. 5–6.

to establish these numbers. What you need to do is the thing you have always needed to do to develop long operational life; that is, to start to develop, to debug, and to build life through use.[42]

Another qualitatively derived function of scale is the external support on which any large public policy enterprise depends for success. Often such support stems, again, from the rising expectations which policy objectives are able to generate. In any case major public approval and the prospect of its continuance is required to render the initial start-up undertakings worthwhile. Such an expensive operation as equipment-intensive research "cannot be turned off and on like a faucet. It must be planned in advance, given adequate lead-time, and funded in such a way that there is assurance that it can move along systematically."[43] As former NASA administrator James Webb noted:

> [a] common denominator of large-scale endeavors is the necessity of a continuing "critical mass" of support. There must be enough support and continuity of support to retain and to keep directly engaged on the critical problems the highly talented people required to do the job, as well as to keep viable the entire organizational structure. . . . Any uncertainty or shortfall in the support factor is apt to have far-reaching effects and force the endeavor into serious difficulties.[44]

Closely related to the public support requirement of large-scale policy objectives is a "capture point" of goal and resource commitment. The meaning and importance of this capture point has been emphasized by Albert O. Hirschman in a study of major development projects in third world nations. In observing these capital and labor-intensive national enterprises, Hirschman notes the extent to which potential project difficulties are underestimated at their outset. He then asserts that for a development project to succeed, "its operators must be 'caught' by the time the unsuspected difficulties appear—caught in the sense that having spent considerable money, time, and energy, and having committed their prestige, they will be strongly motivated to generate all of the problem-solving energy of which they are capable."[45]

Hirschman argues that many agricultural projects fail precisely because they are too short-term and small-scale to reach this capture point and when unanticipated problems arise, they are all too often prematurely abandoned. In effect, they fail because of a reluctance

[42]Silverstein, op. cit., p. 83.

[43]Rosholt, op. cit., p. 88.

[44]Webb, James E., *Space-Age Management: The Large-Scale Approach* (New York: McGraw-Hill, 1969) pp. 62–63.

[45]Hirschman, Albert O., *Development Projects Observed* (Washington, DC: The Brookings Institution, 1967) p. 18.

"to throw good money after what looks like bad, but could be turned into good, if only the requisite rescue effort were forthcoming."[46]

To be sure this policy entrapment effect, as elaborated by Hirschman, is not without its hazards. The attainment of a capture point may well lead after all to the throwing away of good money, time and effort after that which really *is* bad. This, it will be recalled, was the major argument against much of United States military escalation in South Vietnam.

Yet entrapment is important to the large-scale public policy enterprise. It can, for one thing, ensure the continuity of support emphasized by Webb. At the same time, entrapment safeguards the enterprise against many of the uncertainties inherent in its pursuit. In manned space exploration the Kennedy commitment sustained mission goals through even the darkest hours of equipment failures, cost overruns and, ultimately, the tragic spacecraft fire that took the lives of three Apollo astronauts.

Start-Up Administration and Initial Space Decisions

These, then, were the major start-up requisites associated with manned space exploration. They represented, as was noted earlier, major policy thresholds that had to be overcome if any manned missions were to proceed.

In assessing these requisites it is small wonder that a major political commitment, in fact a Presidential mandate, was necessary to energize the manned space exploration program. As was conceded among the emerging career class of space administrators, "science is, and cannot be, the driving force for space exploration."[47] It was President Kennedy's national political commitment which "galvanized the lagging, directionless space effort around a dramatic, not-too-distant goal. . . ."[48]

The full magnitude of the start-up operations to which this chapter has been referring is well illustrated by the budgetary history of the early period of the space program. Figure 2-2 illustrates NASA expenditures from fiscal years 1961 through 1966, highlighting the research and development component of these expenditures.

It is important to note two things about these expenditures: the steeply rising rate of overall space spending and the degree to which R&D-classified outlays approximate the total NASA funds spent.

[46]Ibid., p. 20.

[47]Rechtin, Dr. Everhard, Director, Jet Propulsion Laboratory, California Institute of Technology, in *Hearings Before the Senate Committee on Aeronautical and Space Sciences* (Washington, DC: U.S. Government Printing Office, 1963) p. 138.

[48]Lewis, Richard S., The Kennedy Effect, op. cit., p. 2.

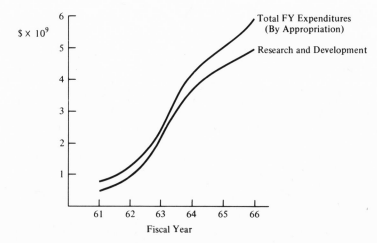

Figure 2-2. NASA expenditures (FY 1961–1966).
Source: Program and Special Reports Division, NASA, July 1971.

Seldom has a government agency increased its appropriations as rapidly as NASA. This strongly reflects the political support associated with the Kennedy moon-landing commitment. But the proportion of R&D expenditures is also revealing. Over 80 percent of NASA funds went into starting up the space exploration enterprise—filling in the gaps in theory, technology and equipment required for manned space exploration to advance. (It is interesting to note by way of contrast that in 1961 only 2.9 percent of the total United States GNP was spent on R&D. In that year the average industry expenditure was 4 percent of sales.)[49]

Another illustration of the dimensions of space exploration start-up is provided by employment data compiled for the 1960–1966 period, shown in Figure 2-3.

This graph, depicting total employment on space exploration programs both within and outside of NASA, emphasizes the personnel mobilization required to pursue space exploration objectives. This manpower pool represents substantial private industrial expansion as well as extensive programs of training and recruitment. It is unlikely that such a work force could have been assembled without the prospect of a major and *continuing* space exploration policy.

With these start-up dimensions of manned space exploration illustrated, it is appropriate to examine briefly the issue of incremental decision making—a model of public policy which has enjoyed a

[49]Hamburg Daniel, *R&D: Essays on the Economics of Research and Development* (New York: Random House, 1966) pp. 13 and 43.

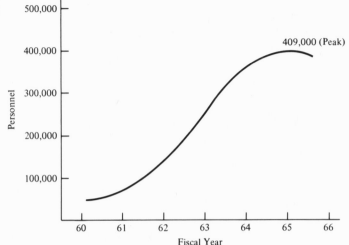

Figure 2-3. Total employment on NASA programs (1960–1966).
Source: Program and Special Reports Division, NASA, July 1971.

wide acceptance since its original formulation by Charles E. Lindblom. Lindblom argues that because of (1) disagreement on primary values and policy objectives and (2) the difficulty of gathering information on which to evaluate a wide range of potential policy outcomes, policy makers typically arrive at their decisions by assessing only "limited comparisons to those policies that differ in relatively small degree from policies presently in effect."[50] He contrasts this behavioral practice with the idealized "synoptic" model of decision making—a model which stipulates that a full range of alternatives are comprehensively analyzed prior to an optimal decision. Lindblom stresses the degree to which short-term commitments and decisional "adjustments" characterize the policy process, and he criticizes efforts at elaborate planning as beyond the bounds of policy-making capability.

Yet what we have so far seen of manned space exploration raises serious exceptions to the application of incrementalism as a paradigm for policy making.[51] The start-up thresholds of the large-scale public policy objective represent problems for which comprehensive (and even optimal) decisions are required. In reviewing the lunar landing program James Webb argued: "We could not stop with doing 80 or 90 or 99 percent of what we needed to do and come

---

[50]Lindblom, Charles E., The 'science' of muddling through, op. cit. p. 84. See also Lindblom and Braybrooke, David, *A Strategy of Decision* (Glencoe, IL: The Free Press, 1963).

out reasonably well."[52] Indeed, for a lunar landing *"a partial success* *is likely to be a complete failure* [emphasis added]"[53]

Additionally, Lindblom asserts that "policy is not made once and for all; it is made and remade endlessly. Policy making is a process of successive approximation to some desired objectives in which *what is desired itself continues to change under reconsideration.*"[54] Yet contrast this with the extended planning and continuity of support so essential to the large-scale policy objective. The long-term lunar landing commitment was the major force supporting the elaborate and expensive start-up undertakings required for space exploration. Manpower training and recruitment closely depended upon the bright future perceived for space programs. Shifts in policy objectives of the sort postulated by Lindblom would, under these circumstances, have proven enormously expensive. They would have seriously undermined the continuity of support which space exploration policy so desperately required.

Finally, the incremental notion of decicion making greatly misrepresents the reality of policy-making thresholds themselves. The consolidation, research, and facilities advancements which this chapter has described were far more than incrementally removed from the policy "state" by which they were preceded. The large-scale policy objective requires radical administrative, psychological and organizational departures if it is to overcome major barriers to its pursuit. These thresholds are policy requirements for which incrementalism is not adequately descriptive.

[51]For other critiques of incrementalism see, form a normative perspective, Dror, Yehezkel, *Public Policy Reexamined* (San Francisco: Chandler, 1968) and Etzioni, Amitai, *The Active Society* (New York: The Free Press, 1968) esp. Chapter 12. For descriptive critiques of the incremental model as it applies to public budgeting see Natchez, Peter B., and Bupp, Irvin C., Policy and priority in the budgetary process, *American Political Science Review*, 67(3) (September, 1973):951–963; Wanat, John, Bases of budgetary incrementalism, *American Political Science Review*, 68(3) (September, 1974) pp. 1221–1228; and Ripley, Randall, and Franklin, Grace A. (eds.), *Policy-Making in the Federal Executive Branch* (New York: The Free Press, 1975) Chapters 3, 4 and 5.

[52]Webb, *Space-Age Management*, op. cit., p. 149.

[53]Idem.

[54]Lindblom, The 'science' of muddling through, op. cit., p. 84.

The Decision-Making Process in Large-Scale Policy

3

Decision making is a process that is inadequately understood. Basically, we know that decisions involve choices among alternatives on the basis of some schemes of assessment and evaluation. In organizational settings, a decision implies the possibility of alternate patterns of collective behavior—the relative probabilities of which can be substantially altered on the basis of a discrimination among them. Within this organizational context, "power" means the ability to select from a set of behavioral possibilities one pattern of action, and to upgrade significantly the chances that the selected pattern will, in fact, result.

But it is important to recognize that the decisional "requisites" outlined above are not automatically forthcoming within organizations. It is distinctly possible that at times the selection of a given alternative will not significantly increase the probability of any consequent organizational action. We generally refer to this as a problem in implementation. Alternatively, it is possible that a significant number of organizational outcomes can occur without benefit of explicit choice. This we call a problem of inadvertence.

Despite these limitations, the decision-making concept has won increased popularity as a focal point for political and policy analysis. Decision-making models have been fashioned to guide research in such diverse subject areas as foreign policy, electoral campaigning, voting, presidential behavior, judicial behavior and a variety of specific public policy issues. Decisions have also been portrayed as the chief responsibility of the organizational executive.[1]

This stress on the decision-making process, while undeniably productive, suffers from a narrowness of scope not generally appreciated. For while decision models have concentrated upon the processes of choice, they have largely ignored the implementation and effects of decisions.[2] If analytical models have been elaborately constructed to portray the conditions, steps and stages leading to a particular alternative's selection, nowhere is there an adequate categorization of the *consequences* of choice. The incremental model, for example, asserts that choice reflects the evaluation of a small range of alternatives, none very far removed from courses of action presently in effect. Yet there is little treatment of the ways in which incremental decisions, once made, differ in their implementation, reversibility or communication and rationalization from other decisions that might be undertaken. Are there, in effect, *types* of decisions that we could usefully identify—not on the basis of the activity which precedes them, but on that which follows? This is a question left unanswered in the present set of decision-making analyses.

This chapter is about the ways in which large-scale policy objectives give rise in their pursuit to two distinctive types of decisions, both identifiable on the basis of peculiar implementation and outcome characteristics. We will term them "go/no-go" and "reflexive" decisions and will examine them in turn.

Largeness-of-Scale and Go/No-Go Decisions

It is time to assert another proposition concerning the large-scale public policy enterprise. *The pursuit of large-scale objectives acts to rigidify many public policy decisions, casting them within an essentially binary go/no-go framework.*

The go/no-go decision is one that must be implemented in its entirety if it is to be implemented at all. It is a decision for which (to

[1]See Simon, Herbert A., *The New Science of Management Decision* (New York: Harper and Brothers, 1966).

[2]For some recent analyses of implementation processes see Pressman, Jeffrey L. and Wildavsky, Aaron, *Implementation* (Berkeley: University of California Press, 1973) and Bardach, Eugene, *The Implementation Game* (Cambridge: M.I.T. Press, 1977).

|44| repeat an earlier phrase) "a partial success is likely to be a complete failure." Go/no-go decisions are highly resistant to incremental adjustments in design and application once undertaken. They act to "lock in" organizational resources, personnel and time schedules to a fixed pattern of implementation.

In manned space exploration, technological imperatives as well as organizational complexity have been major factors in the rigidification of decisions. Much of space programming has been " 'locked up'; it is impossible to change very much without destroying the whole."[3] The incredible number of suboperations that comprise even one major launch program, and their extremely tight interdependence has generally meant that a delay or performance failure in any one area threatens to culminate in a "no-go" for the entire mission.

One illustration of the vast complexity of space programming is afforded in the planning and scheduling method adopted by NASA to structure its missions. Termed NASA-PERT (Program Evaluation and Review Technique), this system is a NASA derivative of one deployed earlier in the Navy Department.[4] Basically, PERT is "a method for integrating the various systems of a project (i.e., spacecraft, launch vehicle, launching support, tracking and data acquisition, etc.) into a coordinated plan."[5] It offers a means by which suboperations can be ordered in time around key organizational events ("milestones") such as contract negotiations, Congressional clearances or public announcements.

The PERT system was established on the recognition "that time, resources and performance specifications are interrelated and can be varied to optimize project plans and development progress."[6] The system employs an elaborate flow chart technique in order to relate these variables.

As utilized in NASA, PERT served to monitor the extremely close interdependency of those operations that comprise the pursuit of a large-scale policy objective. The requirements of these operations, and their mutual satisfaction, establish their own seemingly in-

---

[3]Sayles, Leonard, and Chandler, Margaret, *Managing Large Systems*, (New York: Harper and Row, 1971), p. 23.

[4]For an analysis of the role of PERT in the development of the Navy's polaris missile see Sapolsky, Harvey, *The Polaris System Development: Bureaucratic and Programmatic Success in Government* (Cambridge: Harvard University Press, 1972) Ch. 4. Sapolsky's contention that PERT was of only symbolic significance in the polaris project does not, however, speak to the NASA experience.

[5]*NASA-PERT Handbook*, National Aeronautics and Space Administration (Washington, DC: U.S. Government Printing Office, 1961) p. 1. See also *NASA-PERT in Facilities Project Management*, NASA (Washington, DC: U.S. Government Printing Office, 1965) and Miller, R.W., *How to plan and control with PERT*, *Harvard Business Review* 40 (2) (March/April, 1962): 93–104.

[6]*NASA-PERT Handbook*, op. cit., p. 1.

tractable decision "logic"—a logic of timetables, cost estimates and projected performance levels.

In the most general sense, the Kennedy commitment itself locked NASA into a series of highly rigidified production and testing schedules. One author termed this lock-in the "Kennedy Effect" and blamed it for severely limiting the degrees of decisional freedom open to space policy makers.

> Once the launch vehicle and spacecraft design were decided . . . the Kennedy Effect froze them into a rigid development and testing schedule. Also, it did not allow for any alternative ventures to the moon in the manned program.[7]

Insofar as day-to-day operations were concerned, "the Kennedy Effect produced fabrication and testing schedules which became so rigid that unforseen delays or accelerations of the pace of development had cost increases."[8]

The Kennedy commitment led essentially to a minimum-slack program path. Either all operations along this path had to be relatively successful and on-time or a no-go would result with respect to the lunar landing goal. (The go/no-go nature of NASA operations was closely reflected in the flight testing area where a single no-go would jeopardize the fulfillment of overall mission plans. Under the impact of tight scheduling "an enormous burden was placed on each step in the flight test program. Unless every one was successful, the deadline could not be met."[9])

Yet, as asserted earlier, the Kennedy commitment was essential if manned space exploration was to overcome the inertias and start-up problems that had constrained American advances in the immediate post-Sputnik period. All of this hints at a major space policy dilemma: the very acceleration of expectations and plans required to move space exploration programs forward became a major factor rigidifying the administration of those programs. Each of a series of commitments had to be fulfilled successfully before the next one in sequence could be realized. A less than complete implementation, anywhere along the chain, could threaten the success of an entire project.

This go/no-go characteristic of many space policy decisions is again a quality native to the pursuit of large-scale objectives in general. In fact, a significant insight into the nature of go/no-go deci-

[7]Lewis, Richard S., The Kennedy Effect, *Bulletin of the Atomic Scientists* 24 (3) (March, 1968):4.
[8]Idem.
[9]Lewis, op. cit., p. 5.

sions can be gained from a brief glance at a private policy setting—the well-publicized troubles of the Lockheed Aircraft Corporation over the development of its TriStar 1011 passenger jets.

Scale and the TriStar Dilemma. In 1967 the management of Lockheed committed their company to the construction of 350 L-1011 TriStars. This policy commitment displayed the indivisibility typical of large-scale policy objectives. That is, it required enormous start-up investments; major and confirmed interorganizational support in the form of prepayments from customers, negotiated loans and subcontracts; and, in addition, an explicit commitment to a date for TriStar development and customer delivery.

The Lockheed commitment, because of its scale, began to generate go/no-go decisions of the type outlined above. A tight decisional "logic" emerged, based on the feasibility characteristics associated with the development of the TriStar. Unfortunately, in late 1970 Rolls Royce, Ltd., a subcontractor for the TriStar engine, began to suffer from development problems and cost overruns in the production of its RB 211 power plant. Ultimately, these problems came to threaten the solvency of the company and Rolls was forced to seek British government receivership. As a direct consequence of this difficulty at Rolls, its compliance with Lockheed contract specifications was in doubt.

So rigidified had Lockheed's plans become that any uncertainty in the Rolls production timetable threatened to disrupt the internal logic of the entire TriStar project—forcing it by chain reaction into a no-go, nonoperational state. This, in turn, threatened the continued existence of Lockheed itself.

It is important to note the underlying factors of scale at work in the Lockheed dilemma. Lockheed management was entrapped by its commitment to an indivisible undertaking that became rigidified to the degree that a performance failure in any *one* of its intricate suboperations became critical to the overall project outcome. Further, each operation displayed its own support and commitment imperatives that had to be observed in order to avoid just such a performance failure. Decision logics based upon these imperatives wrested a great number of possible options out of the hands of top level Lockheed management.

The same go/no-go rigidity that lay at the heart of many TriStar development problems, also hindered the efforts of Lockheed executives to rescue the project once its difficulties had begun. Large-scale objectives again revealed their distinctive requirements. As one observer noted:

[It was even difficult] to describe the complexity of . . . [the] task . . . to salvage the TriStar and Lockheed. Nine customers and twenty-four banks had to be kept in the game, if the game were to continue, and all—each with its own needs, interests and responsibilities—had to be convinced that the final deal represented the best possible outcome for them and their stockholders. *All of them had to reach that decision at the same time,* though each preferred to wait until the others had acted [emphasis added].[10]

Lockheed management, of course, had to concede ultimately that a no-go end to the TriStar "game" was beyond their institutional powers to prevent. The company was forced to request a Federal guarantee on a $250 million loan to rescue the TriStar.

In light of this analysis it is interesting to note that extensive criticism of Lockheed executives characterized the Congressional hearings on the loan guarantee. Yet at least some of this criticism might well have been misdirected. Largeness of *scale,* as much as managerial malfeasance, may have been responsible for the TriStar crisis.

The TriStar case illustrates (albeit in a private setting) both the sources and the dangers of those go/no-go decisions that afflict large-scale policy objectives in general. For Lockheed, the close interdependency that existed among a wide variety of operations and organizations was responsible for a foreclosure of TriStar decision options. In manned space exploration the case has proven to be much the same.

Each manned mission has been so extensively planned and is of such technical complexity that there has been little room for flexibility. Major efforts are required for even short-term improvisation. "Tightly interlocked systems are extremely vulnerable; even a single source of difficulty may ruin a program. The Apollo fire of 1967 and the aborted Apollo 13 provide dramatic evidence of this fact. Unbelievably small matters can defeat the mighty."[11]

To be sure, contingency plans have been formulated and redundancies built in throughout space hardware to upgrade the probabilities of successful performance.[12] But contingency plans center primarily around mission aborts, and redundancies are undertaken

---

[10]Meyers, Harold B., The salvage of the Lockheed 1011, *Fortune* 83 (6) (June, 1971):68.

[11]Sayles and Chandler, op. cit., p. 101. For a dramatic account of the "chain reaction" difficulties that threatened the Apollo 13 flight see Cooper, Henry S.F., *Thirteen: The Flight That Failed* (New York: Dial Press, 1973).

[12]For an interesting discussion of the ways in which redundancy and overlapping functions can increase reliability in systems in which they are employed see Landau, Martin, Redundancy, rationality and the problem of duplication and overlap, *Public Administration Review,* 29 (3) (July/August, 1969):346–358.

precisely out of recognition of the small tolerance available for deviation from preestablished performance specifications.

Redundancy, moreover, often leads to decisional rigidity in its own right. Duplication of critical components in space hardware is expensive; once accomplished it must be maintained indefinitely in succeeding generations of equipment to avoid the appearance of slackening safety standards. Thus, once a reliability record has been established, it can act as a inhibiting element in technical innovation and spacecraft redesign. Such was actually the case in early NASA efforts to modify the Army's Redstone rocket for use in the Project Mercury program. Opposition to Redstone modification arose when it was feared that "the Mercury-Redstone was in danger of being modified in about 800 particulars, enough to vitiate the record of reliability established by earlier Redstones and Jupiter-Cs. *Too much redesign also meant reopening the Pandora's box of engineering 'trade-offs,' the compromises between overdesign and underdesign* [emphasis added]."[13]

Additional Go-No-Go Issues. Besides scheduling and reliability logics, largeness-of-scale has imposed upon space policy makers the added psycho-political rigidities that come from the expenditure of massive amounts of public resources. This resource commitment is closely associated with heightened public expectations and elaborately constructed political coalitions—both of which severely limit the degrees of decisional freedom available to space policy makers once major national objectives have been established.

This point needs to be explained further. Frequently, the large-scale policy pursuit is "oversold" to the public in an effort to gain the support and the resources required for it to overcome those "start-up" thresholds described in Chapter 2. Once oversold, it is difficult to modify the basic objectives of the policy by means of subsequent decisions without threatening the political foundations upon which its support has been based. Thus a basic go/no-go situation arises: initial plans must be implemented in their entirety or serious perturbations arise in the alliances formed between the policy bureaucracy and its political supporters. This, of course, is a major reason why the Kennedy moon-landing commitment was *both* the major sustaining and the major constraining factor in the pursuit of American manned space exploration.

A number of bureaucratic factors can likewise preclude the incremental adjustment of large-scale policy decisions once they have

---

. [13]Grimwood, James M., Swenson, Lloyd S., and Alexander, Charles C. *This New Ocean: A History of Project Mercury* (Washington, DC: U.S. Government Printing Office, 1966), p. 181.

been undertaken. First, the scale of policy objectives can enor- mously increase the organizational costs of change. In a large project, change means a much more complex, uncertain series of managerial tasks. Plans and timetables must be redrafted; job assignments are likely to be reshuffled; new employees must be recruited or present employees released. In technology-intensive policy undertakings, such as manned space exploration, the managerial complexity of even the smallest change is heightened dramatically. "Advanced technologies are really tightly knit systems that extend from design and development through to application. Changes ramify quickly and profoundly through the entire system."[14]

Coping with this potential for highly ramified organizational change is not an easy managerial task. This is one reason why bureaucrats seek to avoid adjustments to the decisions that drive the large-scale policy commitment. As one organizational analysis reports: "To make a bureaucracy change its position is much more difficult than allowing it to continue a given policy; the bureaucracy prefers the known dangers of an existing course to the uncertain costs and gains of change."[15]

The "natural" bureaucratic tendency to escape from uncertainty becomes, then, a major factor reinforcing the go/no-go rigidity of large-scale policy decisions. Even small deviations from such decisions threaten an extensive reworking of existing organizational behavior patterns. Organizational routine is at these times often viewed as a precious and highly perishable managerial resource.[16]

Herbert Simon, in *The New Science of Management Decision*, has noted the extent to which routine functions as an escape from the perceived dangers of uncertainty. "A completely unstructured situation," he argues, ". . . is, if prolonged, painful for most people. Routine is a welcome refuge from the trackless forests of unfamiliar problem spaces."[17]

The "vested interests" of bureaucrats themselves reinforce nonadjustive decision making. Organizational decisions, once undertaken, represent assumptions of responsibility (and, in many cases, accountability) on the part of those officials who have played major roles in bringing them about. If such decisions fail to produce desired effects, losses of organizational prestige, if not of positions themselves, can be incurred as a consequence. In this fashion, bu-

[14]Sayles and Chandler, op. cit., p. 39.

[15]Halperin, Morton and Tsou, Tang, "United States Policy Toward the Offshore Islands," *Public Policy* (Cambridge: Harvard University Press, 1966) p. 137.

[16]For the classic treatment of the strategies by which organizations seek to supplant uncertainty with routine see Thompson, James D., *Organizations in Action* (New York: McGraw-Hill, 1967).

[17]Simon, op. cit., p. 39.

reaucrats often develop a major stake in the successful prosecution of those decisions in which they have actively taken part. Reputations and promotions, after all, can rest on the outcome of such ventures.

All of these contribute to an institutionalized *overprotectiveness* of those decisions that key organizational executives are generally known to support. Changes in policy, however small, come to mean admissions of error. Termination of a program amounts to a concession of defeat.

Under these circumstances, it is natural to expect bureaucratic officials to strive mightily to sustain intact those programs with which they are destined to share a familiar fate. Once closely associated with a given decision, an executive must prevent that decision from coming to harm (i.e., "change") in the stages of implementation through which it must pass.

This process of executive overprotection can lock an organization into a rigid decision framework as ruthlessly as can the scheduling or technical factors described earlier. Moreover, overprotection can be particularly acute in the large-scale policy enterprise because the heightened expectations and commitments wrought by scale increase the organizational *consequences* of both success and failure in decision making. As the analyst of one large-scale policy pursuit (the war in Vietnam) describes it:

> Men who have participated in a decision develop a stake in that decision. As they participate in further, related decisions, their stake increases. It might have been possible to dissuade a man of strong self-confidence at an early stage on the ladder of decision; but it is infinitely harder at later stages since a change of mind there usually involves implicit or explicit repudiation of a chain of previous decisions.[18]

At this point it is appropriate to examine some of the implications—both political and organizational—of go/no-go decisions. In a political context, go/no-go decisions are significant. Such decisions are, as we have noted, primarily nonadjustive. They impose a logic upon subsequent organizational action that sharply limits the amount of discretion available to policy managers. Any changes in the basic provisions of the go/no-go decision ramify widely throughout the organizational network that exists for its implementation and, ultimately, the entire decision objective is threatened.

[18]Thomson, James C., "How Could Vietnam Happen? An Autopsy," as quoted in Pfeffer, Richard M. (Ed.), *No More Vietnams?* (New York: Harper and Row, 1968) p. 49. For an additional discussion of psychological factors which can rigidify decision making see Janus, Irving, *Victims of Groupthink* (Boston: Houghton-Mifflin, 1972).

This is hardly an endearing trait to those trained in the com- promise and bargaining processes of politics. It is not easy to reconcile the intractable imperatives of a nonadjustive decision with those shifts in public mood or political coalition to which politicians must be responsive. This incompatibility has led on occasion to conflict in manned space exploration between space policy bureaucrats and Congressional leaders. It has led to friction between NASA and other components of the executive branch.

NASA—Congressional relations on the whole have been good—particularly in the beginning stages of space exploration when public sentiment in support of the Kennedy moon-landing mandate was strong. However, the rigid decisional framework into which many aspects of manned space exploration have been cast has often aroused Congressional suspicions as to the amount of oversight that the Congress could effectively exercise. This revealing exchange between Science and Astronautics Committee member Emilio Daddario and Dr. George Mueller, Director of NASA's Office of Manned Space Flight, took place during a 1967 NASA authorization hearing:

DR. MUELLER: As you know, Mr. Daddario, we have been working very hard to control our costs and live within our budget, and also to live on schedule. . . .

MR. DADDARIO: We recognize your problem, but we have problems of our own. . . . This committee has great faith in you and the explanations you give us. The other day, when you were talking about the future, and the need to keep the program going, the importance of research and development became implicit. Yet . . . in order to meet the present need, the moneys come from research and development. In a sense, there appears to be a conflict. I know you must meet current schedules, but I wonder if by meeting them in this way, we aren't doing more harm than good.

DR. MUELLER: . . . I agree completely with you; it is not in the best interests of the total effort to spend so little money on the space programs. I think we are operating at less than a most efficient level, and that there are real constraints.

On the other hand, we have a clear responsibility and a clear requirement . . . to, in fact, fulfill the committment to land men on the Moon and return them by the end of the decade. We are bending every possible effort to, in fact, accomplish that objective if we humanly can.

MR. DADDARIO: . . . Wouldn't it be better to slow down the present program to place a man on the Moon, and not do harm to your research and development programs and develop, for the future, a greater capability for post-lunar activity.

DR. MUELLER: Mr. Chairman, I am glad you raise that question. We have analyzed this trade-off very carefully and in some depth. . . . We have tried to optimize the selection of the expenditure of funds. . . . It is clear within the period of this decade, the best return on our dollars is accomplished by, in fact, *carrying out the present program and completing it on its present schedule.* [emphasis added][19]

Note the extent to which assessments about the need to maintain preestablished schedules intact dominate the response of the NASA official. It is precisely this inflexibility in manned space programming that has frustrated a number of Congressmen—particularly in recent years when the emotional attachment to space exploration has begun to wane. As one observer complained: "In its relations with Congress, NASA displays a defensiveness which makes it difficult at times for the space committees of the House and Senate to perceive the real problems in the program."[20]

If go/no-go decisions have resulted in strains in NASA–Congressional relations, they have also been the source of conflict between NASA and the executive branch itself. Former President Nixon, for example, demonstrated a great reluctance to sustain NASA budget requests at anywhere near the $5.2 billion annual level at which they peaked in 1965. This brought the President and his Office of Management and Budget into direct conflict with many of those policy imperatives perceived by NASA management.

Internalized executive branch conflicts of this sort even led in 1971 to a rare public criticism by Thomas O. Paine, then NASA administrator of executive office policy, with respect to space exploration budget allocations. In testimony before the Senate Committee on Aeronautical and Space Sciences, Paine announced that, "Speaking very frankly, the NASA fiscal year 1971 authorization and appropriation request is lower than the budget that my colleagues and I would prefer to defend."[21]

But it is not only budgetary cutbacks that rankled NASA adminis-

[19]*NASA Authorization Hearings: Fiscal Year 1967*, Committee on Science and Astronautics, U.S. House of Representatives (Washington, DC: U.S. Government Printing Office, 1966) pp. 531–532.

[20]Lewis, Richard S., The end of Apollo, *Bulletin of the Atomic Scientists* 27(4) (September, 1968):5.

[21]Thomas O. Paine, in testimony during *NASA Authorization Hearings: Fiscal Year 1971*, Committee on Aeronautical and Space Sciences, U.S. Senate (Washington, DC: U.S. Government Printing Office, 1970) p. 20.

trators. A space agency conditioned to operate within binding deci- sional frameworks expressed public resentment over the failure of the Nixon administration to undertake further go/no-go commitments of the type which had propelled space exploration programs in the past. Repeatedly, in Congressional testimony and public statements, NASA officials attempted to prod President Nixon into establishing new manned space missions for the future. On one occasion, a NASA report entered into the transcript of an authorization committee hearing asserted:

> Should the Congress and administration find that additional resources can be made available to NASA, that determination of where and how to apply them *would be contingent upon a clear definition of our national space goals and objectives* and the application of specific priorities. . . .
>
> One urgent area for attention would be manned space flight *where decisions were specifically deferred to President Nixon's administration* [emphasis added].22

Conflicts of this type led ultimately to the resignation of Paine as administrator, and to a subsequent decline in morale among space agency staff in general.

Needless to say, there are abundant economic and political reasons why a President would be reluctant to sustain the space agency in those major commitments to which it had become accustomed. The conflict that nonadjustable decisions precipitate within the executive branch illustrates in part the difficulty of reconciling the "logic" of a large-scale policy with the compromise and bargaining environment of politics.

Scale and Reflexive Decisions

Go/no-go decisions are not the only distinctive variety of decision generated within the large-scale public policy enterprise. Another type is that which we will term the "reflexive decision"—a decision which, in its implementation, materially affects the validity of premises on which it was initially based.

Decisions are constructed around two types of assumptions: those of *desirability* (that is, the goals for which the decision is undertaken) and those of *situation* (that is, the forces at work in determining a perceived condition and the means by which a decision can act upon these forces). Reflexive decisions are ones which,

22Ibid., p. 33.

in their implementation, materially affect the *validity* of those situational assumptions upon which they were based. These premises are then either significantly strengthened in their validity, in which case the decision becomes self-promoting or reinforcing; or they are undermined, which results in a decision that is largely self-frustrating in the achievement of its objectives. We will look at two explanatory examples of reflexive decisions in order to develop the concept more fully.

Reflexive Decisions: Self-Frustrating. Perhaps the most familiar example of the reflexive decision occurs in transportation policy. Recognizing the need to alleviate commuter automobile traffic congestion during rush hour peaks, a number of cities have made decisions to construct elaborate expressway networks connecting the job-dense inner city areas with outlying suburban residential districts. These were decisions undertaken on the premises of projected traffic volume increases and regularized patterns of traffic flow.

Yet the construction of expressway facilities often affected in a causal way the validity of the traffic volume premises upon which expressway decisions were founded. In many cases the facility itself increased traffic volume drastically—sometimes to the extent that an expressway created more congestion than it was designed to alleviate.[23]

Here is an example of decisions that we can describe as reflexive and self-frustrating. They are undertaken on the basis of assumptions that *they themselves invalidate.* Herein lies a distinction between a self-frustrating decision and one which is simply "unsuccessful." An unsuccessful decision may well demonstrate in its implementation that the initial premises upon which it was undertaken were wrong, but it does not in itself *cause* them to be wrong. There is this distinctive feedback associated with the reflexive decision. It is as if the firing of a weapon were the major factor undermining the accuracy of its targeting.

Reflexive Decisions: Self-Promoting. United States military involvement in Vietnam, in one aspect, may offer an all-too-graphic illustration of self-promoting decisions in operation. In 1964, it was decided within the Johnson administration to significantly upgrade the counterinsurgency role of the United States in Vietnam. This was a decision based heavily upon the premise that the Vietcong forces in the South were forming close military alliances with the

---

[23]A Brookings institution study on automobiles and the urban environment concedes that "where all-out efforts are made to accommodate the car, the streets are still congested." See Owen, Wilfred, *The Accessible City* (Washington, DC: The Brookings Institution, 1972).

regular army of North Vietnam.[24] It was a decision that led ulti- mately to major and protracted U.S. military involvement in the Vietnam conflict.

Yet, a number of later analyses have argued that at the time of the U.S. troop commitment decision, North Vietnamese activity in the South was considerably below that level generally assumed by Washington.[25] A plausible case can be made for the U.S. troop commitment as a reflexive, self-reinforcing decision. That is, the troop commitment itself drove the North Vietnamese and Vietcong into closer alliance, encouraging a higher rate of North Vietnamese infiltration into the South. This, of course, reinforced the underlying premises of the troop commitment decision, leading in fact to a series of subsequent decisions in support of the first.

It is deeply significant in this context that the late Senator Robert F. Kennedy came to accuse the Johnson administration of "creating its own reality" in South Vietnam. This is precisely the characteristic of the reflexive, self-reinforcing decision.

Other instances of self-reinforcement readily present themselves: the cumulative effect of individual wage-rate or pricing decisions in the marketplace, for example, which, each undertaken on the basis of anticipated inflationary pressures, collectively create the very inflationary spiral upon which they were predicated; or the nuclear arms race—a sequence of self-reinforcing weapons acquisition decisions each confirming for its architects the reality of enemy belligerence in those responses elicited from the other side.

Having described these two types of reflexive decisions, it is interesting to note the scant attention paid to them in the literature of organization theory and public policy. Reference does appear, on occasion, to the special analytical problems posed by reflexive *predictions*—self-fulfilling or self-frustrating prophecies.[26] Sociologist Robert Merton has analyzed these predictions from a sociological perspective, applying them to race relations where stereotypes often create and sustain their own reality in determining racial behavior.[27] But no analysis is offered within political science of the

[24]See, in this connection, Westmoreland, General William C., "Report on Operations in Vietnam: January 1964–June 1968," in *Report on the War in Vietnam* (Washington, DC: U.S. Government Printing Office, 1968).

[25]See, on this point, Hoopes, Townsend, *The Limits of Intervention* (New York: McKay and Company, 1969) pp. 42, 105, 110; and Buttinger, Joseph, *Vietnam: A Political History* (New York: Praeger Publishing, 1968) pp. 481–488.

[26]See Buck, Roger C., "Do Reflexive Predictions Pose Special Problems for the Social Scientist?" in *The Nature and Scope of Social Science*, edited by Leonard I. Krimerman (New York: Meredith Corporation, 1969) pp. 153–162.

[27]See Merton, Robert K., *Social Theory and Social Structure* (Glencoe, IL: The Free Press, 1968) pp. 421–436. The "circular causation" analysis of racial problems is perhaps most cogently presented in Myrdal, Gunnar, *An American Dilemma: The Negro Problem and American Democracy* (New York: Harper and Row, 1962).

ways in which decisions may feed back on themselves to either enhance or negate the premises upon which they were founded. Complex causal relationships of this type can actually have profound significance for the conduct of public policy. As we will see, they have had an important impact upon manned space exploration.

Reflexive decisions, like their go/no-go counterparts, are closely linked with largeness of scale and, as such, propagate freely within the large-scale public policy enterprise. There is an important reason why this should be so.

Large-scale policy objectives require an extensive amount of interorganizational contact in their pursuit. This contact both enlarges the relevant environment of the enterprise, that is, the range of organizations and interests which can affect or be affected by policy decisions, and at the same time increases the *intensity* with which the environment and policy decisions interact.

In manned space exploration, for example, a wide variety of interest groups, contractors, universities and professional associations are linked to those activities that comprise space policy. These organizations stand to benefit or suffer from space exploration decisions and, consequently, attempt to influence those decisions in favorable directions. Further, many of these organizations stand to benefit or suffer a great deal. They have developed an intensive stake in space exploration policy because the scale of the enterprise increases their dependency on its payoffs. NASA, for example, not only has more contractors than those organizations pursuing small-scale objectives, it also awards considerably *larger* contracts on the average, thus intensifying space policy impacts upon the environment. In the same way a 5 percent layoff of the NASA work force will have a stronger impact upon unemployment statistics than would a 5 percent layoff by a smaller agency.

Thus, not only will more groups be affected by a large-scale policy than by a small one, they are likely to be more intensely affected as well. As James Webb asserted:

> The large-scale endeavor by its very nature—that is, because of its sheer size, its complexity, the investment it requires, the aggregation of power vested in it, and the diverse and highly skilled human resources it must command—necessarily impacts large segments of society with great force.[28]

All of this means that the large-scale public policy enterprise develops a highly interactive relationship with its environment. "The environment is not something apart from the endeavor; it is not just

[28]Webb, James, *Space-Age Management: The Large-Scale Approach* (New York: McGraw-Hill, 1969), p. 109.

something in which the endeavor operates and to which it needs to |57|
adjust; it is an integral part of the endeavor itself."[29]

This tight interactive relationship vastly complicates the causal links between decisions and their outcomes. Like a vast ocean-going vessel, the large-scale enterprise creates extensive turbulence in its wake. Second- and third-order consequences are generated as by-products of action taken toward primary objectives.

The lunar landing commitment, for example, heightened concern in the early 1960s over the supply of scientific manpower in the country at large. It was felt that space-related programs would monopolize the available pool of engineers and technicians to the degree that other efforts in society would suffer. The space program had an intense impact upon scientific and engineering training throughout the country with the result that a technical manpower *oversupply* had been generated by the end of the decade.[30]

These widely ramified consequences of large-scale policy pursuits in general heighten the probability that (1) unanticipated outcomes will occur and, worse, that (2) one or more of these outcomes may materially alter the validity of assumptions upon which a key policy decision relies. This is fertile ground in which to sow the seeds of disaster insofar as organizational guidance is concerned.

Space exploration policy has at times suffered in this exact way from those reflexive decisions it has generated. NASA's problems in land acquisition, for instance, have already been cited in an earlier discussion of the large-scale policy start-up. Decisions to purchase land in the Atlantic Missile Range area led both to major increases in land price and to restrictive changes in land zoning. These changes significantly undermined the cost premises upon which initial purchase decisions had been based, thus rendering land acquisition attempts partially self-frustrating. In a wider sense, it could be argued that NASA's very space exploration success has reflexively frustrated its future attainments. Having achieved and duplicated the feat of a manned lunar landing, public interest in manual space exploration has subsided, and follow-on support to sustain such exploration has dramatically eroded. Here, seemingly, is a case in which a public policy simply "can't win for losing."

Yet, at the same time, space exploration policy has also been aided by reflexive decisions of the self-reinforcing variety. The establishment of specific research programs, for example, often results

---

[29]Ibid., p. 74.

[30]For a treatment of the consequences to the labor force of space exploration programs, as well as the problems besetting technology assessment in general see Bauer, Raymond A., *Second-Order Consequences: A Methodological Essay on the Impact of Technology* (Cambridge: M.I.T. Press, 1969).

in the employment of persons in sufficient numbers that their electoral pressure becomes a major factor in sustaining or enlarging those programs. This, again, is a reflexive arrangement which largeness-of-scale introduces into the conduct of public policy. Because of the size of its commitments, one NASA official admitted: "There is a tendency for our manpower to feed back on us politically—exerting lobbying pressure to maintain space programs." Major weapons development programs in the Department of Defense frequently display this same self-sustaining quality.

Reflexive Challenges to Policy Guidance. Reflexive decisions, of either type, threaten to introduce great uncertainty into the direction and control of large-scale policy. They vastly complicate the relationship between managerial design and policy consequences.

Consider again self-frustrating decisions. Here a policy-making organization is confronted with great challenges regarding goal attainment. Plans themselves may become a major barrier to their own fulfillment. Some organizations under these conditions may be traumatized to eschew comprehensive plans or decisional adjustments of any type given the failures which they can reflexively engender. However, it is also possible that organizations could be tempted by experience with self-frustrating decisions to embark upon the opposite extreme. They may be motivated, that is, to attempt overly ambitious decisional schemes, seduced by the prospect that gaining control over "just one or two more" environmental variables will contain troublesome feedback effects. The land acquisition efforts of NASA, while successful, testify to the way in which reflexivity can escalate organizational decisions.

Meanwhile, the challenges posed by self-reinforcing decisions are scarcely more appealing. These decisions, and the organizations within which they are formulated, amount to self-escalating systems of positive feedback. Such systems diverge sharply in their behavior from the equilibrium processes frequently assumed to characterize policy making. Instead, self-promoting decisions can lead to mutually reinforcing relationships between an organization and its environment—relationships which may not attain balance points or "steady-states."

We will look more closely at the instability of large-scale policy pursuits in the next chapter, but it is important to recognize here that a mutually reinforcing relationship between a policy-making organization and its environment can amount to a system of self-created policy *demand.* Already in public policy settings there are abundant examples of self-created bureaucratic demand. The system of document classification employed in the federal government, for |59| instance, has come to signal importance for those communications included in its coverage. As such, the system has partially created its own artificial document "market"—entirely apart from the national security-related *content* of these documents—thus contributing to the proliferation of government secrecy.[31]

In truth, the implications of self-promoting decisions are enormous. In a world of reflexive policy systems, it may well become impossible to separate analytically the existence of social demands or problems from the "definitions of reality" offered by those organizations that have arisen to deal with them. This means that we cannot arrive at meaningful evaluations of how effectively such organizations are coping with their respective missions because *we cannot assess the dimensions of social need apart from their operation.* The dangers this degree of reflexivity would pose to processes designed to effect control and accountability over public programs are formidable. For democratic political systems, reflexivity problems may well assume urgent proportions.

Taken together, reflexive and go/no-go decisions affect in no small way the control that can be exercised by policy managers over the programs in their charge. Perhaps the most appropriate description of their problem lies in the analogy of the speeding automobile "outrunning" its headlights. As the car gains speed (read: "scale"), it increases its momentum and thus the overall distance that it must utilize to stop or maneuver safely. At a critical velocity it will have extended this distance beyond the illuminating power of its headlights (not to mention the response capabilities of its driver). At this point the forward commitment of the car essentially exceeds the monitoring and corrective capacities of its guidance system.

Reconciling the rigidity of decision logics with the frequent unpredictability of decision performance is a major task confronting the "driver" of the large-scale policy enterprise. It is the *size* of his vehicle, as much as the road over which he travels, that determines those "steering" problems he is likely to encounter.

[31]For a treatment of this aspect of the secrecy problem see Rourke, Francis E., Bureaucratic secrecy and its constituents, *The Bureaucrat* 1 (Summer, 1972): 116–121.

Scale and Instability
in Public Policy

During the mid-1960s, space exploration rode the crest of what amounted to a dynamic and highly complex "policy movement"—a movement consisting of heightened technological and national aspirations, persistent political pressure for Congressional appropriations and seemingly open-ended prospects for original growth. During this period, a "match" was approached in that elusive relationship between public policy and public pressure. Start-up thresholds had largely been overcome and space policy *outputs* (in the form of repeatedly successful manned missions) reached their maximum level of public support.

Yet this match was to be shortlived. As Downs suggests in connection with the "issue attention cycle," public support can quickly subside as the cycle of issue saliency runs its course.[1] This sudden ebb in public pressure can leave a large-scale policy precariously "overscaled" relative to the political resources that exist for its support. It is precisely at this point that the large-scale policy pursuit becomes exceedingly burdensome and vulnerable.

[1]Downs, Anthony, Up and down with ecology—The issue-attention cycle, *The Public Interest* No. 28 (Summer, 1972), pp. 38–50.

As both budgetary and employment data reveal, the sharply ac- |61|
celerating pace of space exploration in the early 1960s gave way
toward the end of the decade to a major decline in policy support,
even before the lunar landing objective was achieved. NASA appropriations declined from $5.2 billion in fiscal year 1965 to $3.0 billion
in 1974. The up and down trends in space funding are revealed in
Figure 4-1, which depicts 1960–1978 NASA appropriations in constant 1967-dollar terms.

Even more dramatic evidence of space policy decline is provided
by the statistics on total personnel employed on NASA programs.
As Figure 4-2 depicts, total manpower dropped from the fiscal year
1965 peak of 409,000 to approximately 126,000 by 1978.

Associated with this personnel and appropriations slide has been
increased public and Congressional criticism of manned space exploration in general, a decline in morale among remaining space
program employees, and specific lapses in organizational perfor-

Figure 4-1. NASA appropriations—FY 1960–1978 (in constant 1967
dollars).

Source: Office of Management Operations, NASA.

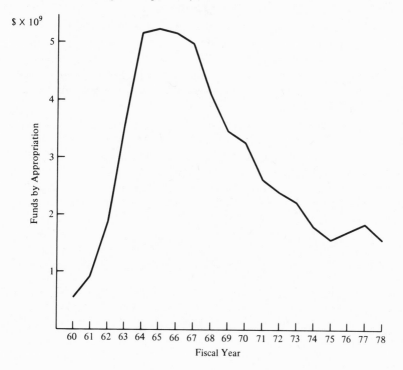

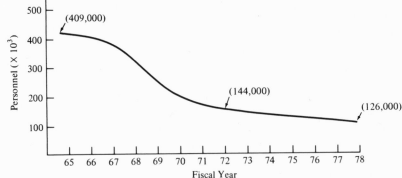

Figure 4-2. Downturn in employment on NASA programs (FY 1965–1978).
Source: Office of Management Operations, NASA.

mance throughout the space policy bureaucracy itself. It is important to examine these latter-year difficulties for they reveal a basic instability associated with large-scale policy making.

The Decline in Space Policy Support

The dawn of the space age was accompanied by a distinct surge of public support. Although survey data during the immediate post-Sputnik period are sketchy, what studies are available suggest both a high degree of worldwide awareness of space events and a subsequent belief that space achievement was in some way linked to national prestige and international power.[2]

Gabriel Almond, in an early survey of opinion in Great Britain, France, Italy, West Germany and the United States, discovered an "extraordinarily high" public recognition of initial satellite launch achievements. "Almost every respondent in the countries surveyed was aware of the launching of the first satellite and of the fact that Russia had launched it. Subsequent awareness of the first American success was also high."[3] This awareness was reinforced by the perceived linkage of space achievement to national strength. As Almond concluded, "One of the most stable popular beliefs of the postwar era—the belief in the scientific and technological superior-

[2]See Almond, Gabriel A., "Public Opinion and the Development of Space Technology," in *Outer Space in World Politics*, edited by Joseph M. Goldsden (New York: Praeger, 1963) pp. 71–96; Michael, Donald N., The beginning of the space age and American public opinion, *Public Opinion Quarterly* 24(4) (Winter, 1960):573–582; and Lott, Albert J., and Lott, Bernice E., Ethnocentrism and space superiority judgments following cosmonaut and astronaut flights, *Public Opinion Quarterly* 27(4) (Winter, 1963):604–611.

[3]Almond, Gabriel, op. cit., pp. 73–74.

ity of the United States—has been rudely shaken, and its place has been taken by anxious estimating that fluctuates with each report of a significant step forward in satellite launchings."[4]

In the United States itself, opinion intensity was high following the Sputnik launches, even though public attitudes were not particularly coherent. "The opinions held by many Americans regarding this first step into space were sometimes inconsistent, occasionally rich in *non sequiturs*, and frequently illogical."[5] Nevertheless, public demand for a space response to the Sputnik achievement was sharp. A Survey Research Center poll conducted shortly after Sputnik reported that "77 per cent thought that the Russian satellite should make 'a difference in what we are doing about the defense of this country', with . . . 47 per cent going for a crash program on weapons development."[6]

These defense-related assessments of the importance of space exploration heightened the sense of urgency surrounding United States entry into the "space race." The Kennedy commitment translated this sense of urgency into political commitments leading in a civilian direction.[7] It was this civilian policy response, however, that did not wear well in terms of public support.

As early as 1965, Gallup polls began to indicate softening of both public interest and support where expensive, nonmilitary space exploration undertakings were concerned. A July 1965 poll revealed a 36 percent preference among those contracted for decreased space exploration expenditures, as against 42 percent in favor of keeping these expenditures the same, and 16 percent in support of their increase.[8]

Even more dramatic evidence of diminishing public space policy support is provided in a 1967 Gallup poll. Here, in response to the question, "Do you think it is important or is not important to try to send a man to the moon before Russia does?", 60 percent of those interviewed assessed the landing race as not important.[9]

By February 1969, 40 percent of Gallup poll respondents called for a reduction in space research expenditures as against 41 percent approving present levels of those expenditures.[10] In addition, a July 1969 poll (on the threshold of the lunar landing) revealed that 53

[4]Ibid, p. 77.
[5]Michael, Donald N., op. cit., p. 581.
[6]Ibid, p. 579.
[7]See Van Dyke, Vernon, *Pride and Power: The Rationale of the Space Program* (Urbana, IL: University of Illinois Press, 1964); and Logsdon, John M., *The Decision to Go to the Moon: Project Apollo and the National Interest* (Cambridge: M.I.T. Press, 1970).
[8]Gallup Opinion Index, No. 3 (August, 1965) p. 16.
[9]Gallup Opinion Index, No. 22 (April, 1967) p. 19.
[10]Gallup Opinion Index, No. 45 (March, 1969) p. 17.

percent of those interviewed opposed a Mars manned landing as a follow-on project to the Apollo program. Only 39 percent favored such a goal.[11]

This erosion of public support for space policy was closely related to increased criticism of NASA programs and their expenditure requirements. A number of Congressional critics began to question the "pork barrel" distribution of NASA facilities. (This distribution was apparent from the outset of the space race. Supposedly, New York Senator Kenneth Keating even "kept a monthly account of the 'share' his state received compared to California and New Jersey.")[12] Public debates also began over the relative merits of manned versus unmanned flight. Such debates were particularly heated at times of NASA setbacks or Soviet achievements in purely instrumented flight.

National opinion leaders, such as Senator Edward Kennedy and the Reverend Ralph Abernathy, began to speak out against space exploration as a diversion of scarce national resources that were urgently needed elsewhere. Space exploration came to be viewed in other circles as an extension of military and defense policy making and it was opposed on this basis.[13] Finally, "counterculture" values among a significant portion of the young condemned space exploration as an extravagant exercise in "mindless technology."

This increased opposition to space exploration led to serious declines in morale within the space policy bureaucracy. Manpower layoffs coupled with the failure to establish follow-on goals contributed to the notion that the future was "running out" on the space program. This perception, in turn, aggravated latent scientist–engineer controversies within NASA. The prospects of limited flight opportunity intensified feelings of discrimination on the part of scientist–astronauts who had lost out in competition with pilot–astronauts in past mission assignments and for whom few future space flight opportunities seemed to remain.[14]

The vision of a limited future profoundly influenced the degree of enthusiasm and commitment which space personnel brought to their work setting. As one former NASA official asserted: "If the economy were to improve and jobs open up elsewhere, NASA would really decline."

[11]Gallup Opinion Index, No. 50 (August, 1969) p. 20.

[12]Diamond, Edwin, The Rise and Fall of the Space Age (New York: Doubleday and Company, 1964) pp. ix–x.

[13]See Etzioni, Amitai, The Moon Doggle (New York: Doubleday and Company, 1964), and Melman, Seymour, Pentagon Capitalism (New York: McGraw-Hill, 1970).

[14]See NASA: Trouble in paradise, Newsweek 74 (September 22, 1969): 73–74; and Trouble at NASA: Space scientists resign, Science 165 (August 22, 1969): 776–779.

Declines in Organizational Performance

The sense of decline that developed within the space policy bureaucracy also had important consequences for the policy effectiveness of that organization in the attainment of its objectives. Specific problems emerged in organizational performance, some of which are highly significant given the close ranges of tolerance upon which successful space exploration missions depend.

Declines in Employee Capability. One source of difficulty in pursuing space programs has stemmed from the movement of highest quality personnel out of NASA into areas of greater perceived excitement and opportunity. In recent years, despite indifferent or distinctly unfavorable job markets, much of NASA's most valuable scientific and managerial talent has left the agency for brighter prospects in universities, private industry or alternate government agencies, such as the Department of Energy or National Science Foundation. This exodus has left the space program without some of its most imaginative and capable personnel. Many of these individuals were among the space agency's most important assets. As one former NASA official phrased it in a private interview:

> Programs like Apollo attract people who like challenges. Once the major problems are solved these people are no longer interested. Those left behind are really mediocre, and they establish a self-fulfilling mediocrity within the program.

This loss of outstanding scientific and managerial talent acts in a general sense to diminish prior levels of organizational adaptability and problem-solving effectiveness.

Emerging Problems in Quality Control. One of the most consistent areas of concern throughout the history of the space program has been that of hardware reliability and quality control (R&Q). The "methodology" of quality control became the subject of intensive debate immediately on the formation of NASA and its first undertakings in the planning of manned space flight.[15] Among the major factors fueling this debate were the extraordinarily high performance expectations and safety standards applied to hardware involved in manned missions. The following mission and human safety reliability goals,[16] among many proposed early in the Project

---

[15]See Grimwood, James M., Swenson, Lloyd S., and Alexander, Charles C., *This New Ocean: A History of Project Mercury* (Washington, DC: U.S. Government Printing Office, 1966) pp. 178–190, 265–268.

[16]Ibid., p. 182.

Mercury program, illustrate the performance standards expected from the new space flight technology. These goals are expressed as success probabilities, predicated on the probability theory assumption that total system reliability is the product of component reliabilities within that system.

Mission Phase	Mission Success Reliability	Human Safety Reliability
Boost	.7917	.9963
Orbit	.9890	.9999
Retrograde	.9946	.9946
Reentry	.9992	.9992
Overall	.7781	.9914

The figures above represent exceptionally high reliability aspirations given their computation on the basis of *multiplied* (and not simply additive) failure potentials.

Aspirations such as these led to careful attention on the part of space policy planners to ways in which organizational capacities for quality control could be maximized. Extensive debate erupted over the extent to which quality control was to be a technologically or a psychologically derived organizational characteristic. That is, was the precision and reliability required in the manufacture of space flight hardware best obtained by new production line technologies or by structuring employee motivation in the direction of error-free performance? These debates even spilled over into the basic concepts of manned space flight itself. Was man along on space missions simply to upgrade reliability in basically automated flight control systems, or were these systems to be backup devices designed to supplement the primary control of man? Was man or machine, in the final assessment, the major source of mission reliability?

While wrestling with these questions, NASA attempted to upgrade both human and technological reliability. Ultimately, however, space mission designers came to operate under the assumption that man was the final guarantee of space flight success. Manual overrides were built into almost all automated flight control systems, and critical go/no-go "decision points" were structured into missions and reserved for judgment by man—whether he be in a space capsule or in a ground controlling station. NASA stressed publicly (often in answer to its critics) the importance of man to space flight—both as an efficient source of mission guidance and as a highly adaptive and flexible instrument for coping with the unexpected.

At the same time, in spacecraft production NASA and its contrac- tors have strongly recognized the role of "human factors" in quality control. Employee motivation is considered a primary element in the care and workmanship accorded the manufacture of space hardware.

Space flight equipment, of course, requires the greatest technical precision in both its design and manufacture. The image of the "white room" with its sterilized, dirt-free environment has come to characterize the "assembly line" of the space age. Yet behind the elaborate rules and assembly procedures, the monitoring and testing technology, is recognition of the fact that no matter how detailed or sophisticated the safeguards "if the employee doesn't care whether or not he makes a mistake, he will probably err."[17]

Operating under this assumption (for which a significant amount of investigative support exists),[18] NASA has carefully developed programs to add a motivational component to quality control. Apollo, Skylab and future space shuttle astronauts have made repeated visits to divisional offices, contractors and subcontractors in order to upgrade the morale of space employees by increasing their sense of importance and identity with respect to space exploration programs. The lunar landing commitment itself provided a major incentive for extra care in spacecraft assembly. Workers on Apollo hardware felt a special motivation to sustain the quality of their job performance as a means of personal participation in an endeavor of historic proportions.

Yet, along with the decline in public support and employee morale that beset the space policy bureaucracy, an erosion occurred in quality control capability. One NASA official privately conceded that in Apollo "the number of anomalies [rose] alarmingly in each successive flight after [Apollo] 11." Another reported that with this erosion "worries about quality have become a fetish with higher management."

There is a great deal of importance to these statements. Apollo 11 was the first lunar landing mission. It marked the fulfillment of that commitment to which most of NASA's activities over the decade of the 1960s had been dedicated. At the same time, it represented the end of a period of clear direction for space exploration policy. One goal had lapsed and no new ones appeared to take its place.

[17]Halpin, James F., *Zero Detects: A New Dimension in Quality Assurance* (New York: McGraw-Hill, 1966) p. 3.

[18]See, for example. Harris, Douglas H. and Chaney, Frederick B., *Human Factors in Quality Assurance* (New York: Wiley, 1969) and Rook, R. C., *Motivation and Human Error* (Albuquerque: Sandia Corporation, 1965).

It is quite likely that this lack of direction contributed to NASA's problems with respect to quality control. Without the espirit that characterized the space "challenge" of the early 1960s, there was a lapse in what might be described as the organizational "will to be careful." This would at least partially explain why failures or "gliches" occurred with increasing frequency even in basically tried and tested spacecraft systems.

It is understandable that unexpected problems would occur in first-time equipment such as the lunar rover. But when anomalies develop in "standard" hardware, the construction of which has been established on a repetitive basis, a decline in organizational morale can certainly be suspected. A development that seems to fly in the face of common sense—"practice" making for increasingly imperfect manufacturing results—would seem at least partially explained as a natural tendency for carelessness to develop among employees once a sense of challenge or importance disappears from the work setting.[19]

Related Declines in Organizational Structure

At the same time, related decays began to develop in the structure of the space policy bureaucracy itself. An organizational fragmentation and contraction hit the space program and threatened to move it in the direction of the inchoate administrative arrangements that characterized the immediate post-Sputnik period. Appropriations and manpower cutbacks were, of course, crucial in this but, again, a major source of trouble lay in the failure to establish follow-on goals to the manned lunar landing.

One important structural decay in the space policy bureaucracy has been the dismemberment of many university laboratories from the organizational framework of the space program. Cutbacks in NASA's training grants and the elimination of its Sustaining University Program pushed a number of university laboratories out of their involvement with space exploration.[20] Those laboratories that remained attached to the program found the general decline in NASA's experimentation interest a deeply disturbing development. "Several laboratories which . . . evolved sophisticated techniques of manufacturing their own instruments and . . . brought together talented technical teams now faced the prospect of losing these

[19]For an interesting discussion of general responses to decline in organizations, see Hirshman, Albert O., *Exit, Voice and Loyalty: Responses to Decline in Firms, Organizations and States* (Cambridge: Harvard University Press, 1970).

[20]See, in this connection, Lambright, W. Henry and Henry, Lauren L., Using universities: The NASA experience, *Public Policy* 20(1) (Winter, 1972): 61–82.

resources."[21] The lapse in space exploration goals continues to |69|
render the future of university laboratories in space exploration
uncertain.

The dilemma of the laboratories is that they require lead time of 18
months to two years to develop instrumentation for satellite experiments and to train graduate students to handle the data. With nothing
in the offing they can count on . . . they are having a difficult time
maintaining a trained laboratory staff and keeping students on tap.[22]

Besides university laboratories, a number of smaller aerospace contractors have either dissolved under the impact of space appropriations cutbacks or have run into serious trouble to the extent of their
dependence upon space contract revenue. Other former contractors
have detached themselves from space exploration assignments in
favor of more promising long-term prospects elsewhere.

Even major NASA contractors have not escaped internal upheav-
als as a result of fiscal and manpower retrenchment. Shrinkage of
the aerospace industry has raised the prospect "that the . . . manufacturing and testing establishment developed to build Apollo will
fall apart."[23]

The Instability Dilemma in Manned Space Exploration

These space exploration declines—in public support, appropriations,
manpower, morale, organizational structure and organizational
performance—all illustrate a fundamental characteristic of the
large-scale policy enterprise. *Largeness-of-scale acts to destabilize
public policy, depriving it of middle ground between self-
generating states of growth and decay.* Large-scale policy pursuits
are not likely to realize a point of equilibrium or "steady state"
between support-mobilizing expansion and downward spirals of disillusionment and decline. There is perhaps nothing space exploration demonstrates more persuasively than this very point.

Requiring initially a major goal-oriented thrust to overcome organizational start-up requirements, space exploration soon developed a momentum of its own based on heightened aspirations
and the need to cope with long developmental lead times by means
of long-range plans. Ultimately, shortfalls developed in both political commitment and public support, and instead of stabilizing at a

[21]Richard S. Lewis, Goal and no goal: A new policy in space, *Bulletin of the Atomic Scientists*
23(5) (May, 1967):19.

[22]Idem.

[23]Lewis, Richard S. Our terra–lunar transit system: Where will it take us? *Bulletin of the
Atomic Scientists* 25(3) (March, 1969): 22.

point of minimal growth, space exploration policy began rapidly to decay downward in appropriations, manpower and organizational structure and performance. A self-supporting decline came to grip the space program in the same way as a missile itself plummets to earth after failing to achieve escape velocity.

In its stages of decline, space exploration began to fall below some of the very thresholds it had surpassed in attaining its original start-up. The organizational edifice wrought by administrative consolidation and external institutional support first began to break apart. It was closely followed by a psychology of falling fortunes and a near return to the conservatism that had characterized space exploration prior to the lunar landing commitment. "In contrast to the exhuberance and sense of mission which characterized the beginning of Apollo, NASA leaders [came to] exhibit *the indifference to advanced projects that characterized the Eisenhower administration's attitude toward manned flight beyond Earth orbit,* [emphasis added]."[24]

Here, then, is the basic instability dilemma associated with manned space exploration. It represents a policy enterprise not susceptible to balance between forces pushing for its enlargment and those moving it toward decay. Space exploration capabilities "are highly perishable unless they are used; they cannot be mothballed or put on a shelf, or placed on a standby basis. *They require a critical mass of activity or they will rapidly disintegrate* [emphasis added]"[25]

This is, of course, why the presence of explicit goals has been of such commanding importance to the space policy bureaucracy. As NASA deputy administrator Robert C. Seamans contended in 1968: "Our course for the period beyond this decade must now be set or we must commence the abandonment of the capability that we have created."[26]

This instability creates extensive managerial problems for those who would direct space programs. Reconciling the "imperatives" of space policy to the compromise and bargaining processes of politics is, as was discussed earlier, a task of major dimensions. When, however, an entire policy *in itself* is devoid of middle ground on which to "ride out" shifts in political attitudes or coalitions; when it will not permit "holding actions" during times of turbulence with respect to its support, the prospects for successful management appear slim at

[24]Lewis, Richard S., The end of Apollo, *Bulletin of the Atomic Scientists*, 24(7) (September, 1968): 4.

[25]Harvey, Mose L., "The Lunar Landing and the Soviet Equation," in *Man on the Moon*, edited by Eugene Rabinowitch (New York: Harper and Row, 1969) p. 71.

[26]Seamans, Robert C., Jr., as quoted in Lewis, Goal and no goal, op. cit., p. 18.

best. James Webb, perhaps the most successful of NASA administrators, described from his perspective the instability dilemma in
large-scale management:

> The process of management in the large-scale endeavor becomes that
> of fusing at many levels a large number of forces, some countervailing,
> into a cohesive but *essentially unstable* whole and keeping it in mo-
> tion in a desired direction [emphasis added][27]

The instability wrought by scale is also the subject of the following
managerial assessment:

> The administrator of the large-scale system works to control it to the
> point where he can concentrate on forward direction of its missions.
> He recognizes that he will always be working with a *relatively unsta-
> ble system*, and he seeks controls that will override the potentially
> detrimental effects of this built-in instability [emphasis added][28]

Recognizing the exceedingly thin margins between policy expansion
and decay, space exploration managers have exhibited an impressive
resourcefulness in attempting to maintain growth in their programs.
Both Soviet and American space administrators, for example, have
repeatedly praised the achievements of the other side in an effort to
generate competitive spirit for increased efforts at home.[29] In the
early 1970's, as the enthusiasm for international competition had
waned, NASA officials stressed the possibilities of international
cooperation in space as an incentive to the Nixon and Ford administrations to upgrade space funding. As one astute observer at the time
described it:

> The reasoning goes like this: If NASA could establish an opportunity
> for improved Soviet–American relations through cooperation in
> space, this would presumably create the need for a series of Post-
> Apollo missions of historic proportions. Considering the current poli-
> tics of detente with the big powers, it would be hard for the White
> House or Congress to say no to funds for such an effort.[30]

The Apollo–Soyuz joint orbital flight, first announced during
former President Nixon's Moscow summit, testifies to at least the
partial success of this approach.

Yet when strategies as circuitous as these have not met with
success, NASA leaders have not failed to resort to more direct

[27]Webb, James E., *Space-Age Management* (New York: McGraw-Hill, 1969) pp. 135–136.
[28]Sayles, Leonard, and Chandler, Margaret, *Managing Large Systems* (New York: Harper and Row, 1971) p. 104.
[29]See, on this point, Rourke, Francis E., *Bureaucracy and Foreign Policy* (Baltimore: The Johns Hopkins Press, 1972) pp. 47–48.
[30]Wilford, John Noble, Cooperation in space, *The New York Times* (December 6, 1971).

methods. Most of these efforts, as described in the preceding chapter, have taken the form of public pronouncements designed to pressure the President into adopting new commitments toward which the declining space policy bureaucracy could be directed.

Skylab and the Apollo Applications Program

To describe the instability dilemma associated with manned space exploration is not to deny that efforts have been made to find a steady-state basis on which to maintain space programs. The Apollo Applications and Skylab projects were both attempts to locate that intermediate ground upon which space organization and appropriations could be stabilized. Skylab, in particular, was conceived as a balanced, well-paced series of orbital experimentation missions—a "holding program which keeps the technology alive, but barely so, until the nation recovers its interest in new frontiers and decides to become venturesome again."[31] But Skylab, at its outset, suffered in competition with the Army's Manned Orbiting Laboratory (MOL) program. Those Skylab missions that were conducted suffered from a public disinterest as well as from manufacturing flaws in the Skylab itself. Ironically, it was the disintegration of Skylab, in a fiery reentry, that brought it most to public attention.

Another stabilization effort, the Apollo Applications Program (AAP) failed dramatically to elicit the enthusiasm necessary to counterbalance the costs involved in its undertaking. In a study of post-Apollo planning in NASA, Emmette Redford and Orion White reported that "the AAP program remained throughout its development in a highly fluid state, without objectives ever being firmly decided upon."[32] They conclude that:

> ... the AAP, after being squeezed into acceptable dimensions by NASA's top leadership, the Bureau of the Budget, and the Congressional budget process, would have been given adequate support if it had not run into competition with other demands on national resources. What mainly brought it down ... was apparently the budgetary stringency produced by the Vietnam war, the Great Society program, the riots in the cities and the fear of continued inflation.[33]

In this conclusion, however, Redford and White ignore the nonincremental and indivisible nature of space exploration as a

---

[31]Lewis, The end of Apollo, op. cit., p. 5.

[32]Redford, Emmette S. and White, Orion F., *What Manned Space Program After Reaching the Moon? Government Attempts to Decide: 1962–1968* (Syracuse: The Inter-University Case Program, 1971) p. 140.

[33]Ibid., p. 223.

large-scale policy pursuit. It is equally plausible that what really |73| destroyed the Apollo Applications program was its very *formulation* as an incremental and balanced policy alternative. Once "squeezed into acceptable dimensions," it lost the persuasive *content* that would have justified its proposed expenditures. This is precisely the problem that largeness-of-scale introduces into the development of public policy. Without major mobilizing commitments (such as landing a man on the moon and returning him safely), large-scale objectives simply cannot generate and sustain the support required for their successful pursuit.

A deep-seated paradox is at work here. In order to fit comfortably into an incremental framework, the AAP was cast in a form that was basically *not large enough* to be persuasive. Then, without being able to generate its own political commitment, the AAP suddenly became *too large* for available amounts of public support.

All of this hints again at the thresholds associated with the large-scale policy enterprise. There are distinct mileposts or points-of-scale at which qualitative shifts occur in both political support and policy performance. Early in this analysis of manned space exploration we described start-up thresholds that existed with respect to organizational development and administrative consolidation. At the same time, support and commitment thresholds were noted as part of the large-scale policy start-up as well. (Commitments and plans, that is, had to be large if they were also to be persuasive.) Now it is appropriate to note that thresholds of this type are important to policy *maintenance* as well as start-up. This is why growth is so important to the large-scale policy undertaking. Large-scale policy must continue to mobilize extensive support and enthusiasm if its extensive costs are to be deemed worthwhile.

As has been said, manned space exploration constituted at its height a policy "movement" fueled by high aspirations, public pressures and seemingly open-ended prospects for organizational growth. Significantly, instability is a major characteristic of social movements generally.[34] They must mobilize increasing numbers of persons to their support or they risk disintegration and decay. At the other extreme, the very success of social movements can jeopardize their continuance insofar as success leads to institutionalization and their crystallization in bureaucratic form. In this connection, Hannah Arendt has noted "the perpetual motion mania of totalitarian movements which can remain in power only so long as they

---

[34]From the well-developed literature that exists on social movements, see especially Cantril, Hadley, *The Psychology of Social Movements* (New York: Wiley, 1941); King, C. Wendell, *Social Movements in the United States* (New York: Random House, 1956); and Arendt, Hannah, *The Origins of Totalitarianism* (New York: Harcourt, Brace and World, 1966).

keep moving and set everything around them in motion."[35] She contends that totalitarian regimes, "if they do not pursue global rule as their ultimate goal . . . are only too likely to lose whatever power they have already seized."[36]

Note the striking similarity here between Arendt's description (to the extent that it may be correct) of totalitarian movements and the instability dilemma of the large-scale policy enterprise. Both require an extensive mobilization of public resources or support for their start-up. Both must then *maintain* this mobilization above a critical level or they will rapidly disintegrate. Finally, both require the presence of expansive goals as the primary means of protecting this critical mass of support.

In this connection, Albert Hirschman has noted that "the promise of some sort of utopia is most characteristic of larger-scale undertakings such as the launching of social reforms or external aggression because they are likely to require heavy initial sacrifices."[37] Utopian promises (and sharply rising expectations) in themselves contribute to explosive social instability; they are not likely to lead to public policies which are readily susceptible to balance or long-term steady states.

Instability and the Space Shuttle Commitment

These dilemmas faced by manned space exploration policy managers in sustaining their programs have certainly not gone unheeded by top leadership in either the aerospace industry or the White House. NASA, of course, has targeted many of its public pleas for support directly toward Presidential ears. Important Congressional and industry pressure has also been brought to bear for the upgrading of space exploration policy goals.

In response to growing pressures, in 1969 former President Nixon appointed a special Space Task Group, consisting of Vice President Agnew, Science Advisor Lee A. Dubridge, Air Force Secretary Robert C. Seamans and NASA Administrator Thomas O. Paine, to assess follow-on goals for space exploration. The Task Group urged the adoption of a Mars manned landing goal, but at a "moderate pace." No specific date and no overriding national priority were to be attached to the endeavor.[38] Yet the President was not willing to

---

[35]Arendt, *Origins of Totalitarianism*, op. cit., p. 306.
[36]Ibid., p. 392.
[37]Hirschman, Albert O., *Development Projects Observed* (Washington, DC: The Brookings Institution, 1967) p. 31.
[38]See "The Post-Apollo Space Program: Directions for the Future," *Space Task Group Report to the President* (Washington, DC: U.S. Government Printing Office, 1969).

make any political commitment of this order, and efforts were con- |75| tinued toward finding some middle ground upon which space exploration policy (and expenditures) could unobtrusively rest.

As pressure built and organizational decay continued, however, even a highly cautious Nixon could not escape the imperatives of the large-scale policy enterprise. On January 5, 1972, the President authorized the National Aeronautics and Space Administration to undertake development of a partially reusable space "shuttle"— designed for near-space transit and projected to cost approximately $5.5 billion within a six-year time frame.[39]

The space shuttle commitment represented an expansive goal with which to upgrade once again the manned space exploration program. Yet the shuttle represents at the same time a goal to change the nature of space exploration policy—*to transform it from a large-scale to a divisible organizational pursuit.* Proponents of the shuttle describe it as

> ... a whole new way of spaceflight—nonpilots in space, multiple payloads that could be placed where they were wanted or picked up out of orbit; new designs of satellites, free from the expensive safeguards against the vibrations and shocks of launch by rocket. Costs of putting a pound of payload in orbit should drop by one half, from $200 to $100.[40]

These space flight alternatives would begin to allow diverse and specialized payoffs to multiple constituencies from space programming. As such, space policy would be freed from many of the threshold effects which have characterized it in its large-scale phase. Benefits could be derived in relationships proportionate to resource commitments, allowing for balance and pluralist adjustment processes in policy making.

It is possible in this way for a large-scale policy pursuit to transform itself into a conventional one provided there is an alteration in the indivisibility requisites attached to its feasibility. For space exploration, the transformation depends upon altering the *technology* of flight—changing its character from "prescriptive" (requiring major sunk costs and careful planning) to "adaptive" (low in unit costs and flexible in application).[41]

[39]See *The Washington Post* (January 6, 1972), p. 1; and Mathews, Charles W., Deputy Administrator for Manned Space Flight, NASA, "The Space Shuttle and Its Uses," paper delivered at Symposium on World Space Projects, Royal Aeronautical Society, London, England, April 21, 1971.

[40]Anderson, Frank W., Jr., *Orders of Magnitude: A History of NACA and NASA, 1915–1976* (Washington, DC: U.S. Government Printing Office, 1976) p. 94.

[41]For a description of these technology types see Zwerling, Stephen, *Mass Transit and the Politics of Technology* (New York: Praeger, 1974) pp. 12–15.

Significantly, however, this transformation is *itself* large-scale in its requirements. The shuttle is predicated on the existence of a transformation threshold. Extensive investment must be made now in space craft development in order to reduce sharply space flight costs in the future.[42]

In a general sense, the space shuttle has been a political commitment, issued and upheld by reluctant Presidents, to rescue the space policy bureaucracy from the decay spiral in which it had been caught. "The move to develop the shuttle strengthens the shrinking aerospace industry and keeps the United States in manned space flight during the critical years of the post-Apollo . . . period."[43] As such, it testifies graphically to the dilemma of large-scale policy undertakings unable to sustain themselves in a steady state.

[42]For a review of arguments both for and against the space shuttle see Holman, Mary A., *The Political Economy of the Space Program* (Palo Alto: Pacific Books, 1974) and Levine, Arthur L., *The Future of the U.S. Space Program* (New York: Praeger, 1975).

[43]*The Washington Post*, op. cit., p. 1.

The Politics of Mismatched Scales: A Sketch of the War on Poverty

5

No analysis of large-scale policy could be complete if founded upon an explication of manned space exploration alone. While space exploration reveals the attributes of large-scale objectives in unfettered pursuit, it fails for precisely this reason to portray the more frequent political environments that surround these objectives. It is not, after all, bureaucratic detachment, extensive political mobilization and free-flowing resources which characterize most public policy undertakings. Instead, it is fleeting public attention, elaborately constrained resources and competitive intrusions upon organizational jurisdictions that define the political order of the day.

These are the very conditions to which large-scale policy undertakings are exceedingly vulnerable. In confrontation with conventional pluralist processes the development and output of large-scale policy can look very different as we will see from the pattern evidenced in space exploration.

As was mentioned at the outset of this study, large-scale policy objectives do not imply the existence of congruently large frameworks of organization and commitment. Conversely, the presence of such frameworks does not guarantee the pursuit of large-scale policy. Perhaps no better illustration of the first condition can be found than in the design and prosecution of the war on poverty in the 1960s. The examination offered here will not be exhaustive. It is designed instead to highlight the ways in which the implicit scale characteristics of poverty policy objectives confronted an essentially uncongenial political and organizational environment.

The Poverty Policy Start-up

The war on poverty began in a fashion not unlike the acceleration assocaited with manned space exploration—with an explicit Presidential mandate. On January 8, 1964, President Lyndon B. Johnson, in his first State of the Union address, announced to the nation: "This Administration today, here and now, declares unconditional war on poverty in America. I urge this Congress and all Americans to join with me in this effort." "Our aim," the President continued, "is not only to relieve the symptom of poverty, but to cure it, and above all, to prevent it."[1]

The President shortly after reinforced his "declaration of war" with a special message to Congress outlining the provisions of an Economic Opportunity Act. "I have called for a national war on poverty," Johnson reminded the Congress. "Our objective: total victory." The President described the act as a "total commitment by this President, and this Congress, and this nation, to pursue victory over the most ancient of mankind's enemies."[2]

Again, as in the case of manned space exploration, it is instructive to review earlier efforts to cope with poverty problems prior to the casting of poverty policy in President Johnson's expansive terms. Prior to the Johnson commitment, little in the way of antipoverty policy was pursued among governmental agencies. To be sure, a patchwork of assorted public assistance and income support programs existed at federal and state governmental levels directed towards ameliorating the effects of poverty, but no public undertakings were directed toward systematically identifying and attacking the *causes* of poverty.[3] Indeed, much of the ancestry of the war on poverty lies in the private sector—in the "Grey Areas Program" of the Ford Foundation.

An experimental program of the late 1950s, the Gray Areas proj-

---

[1]*Public Papers of the Presidents, Lyndon B. Johnson, 1964* (Washington, DC: U.S. Government Printing Office, 1965) p. 114.

[2]Ibid, pp. 376; 380.

[3]Anderson, James E., Brady, David W., and Bullock, Charles, *Public Policy and Politics in America* (North Scituate, MA: Duxbury Press, 1978) p. 132.

ect was designed to effect slum rejuvenation in several major cities. It operated under the assumption that "rehabilitation of slum areas requires institutional changes including governmental reorganization."[4] In addition to the Ford Foundation, the President's Committee on Juvenile Delinquency and Youth Crime, formed in 1961, was also involved in antipoverty efforts—offering small grants to local communities for youth opportunity programs.

In these early days, antipoverty efforts lay essentially within the province of a technical elite of foundation officials, business leaders and social scientists, largely detached from formal policy-making institutions. In addition, unlike the case of manned space exploration, there did not exist a corpus of formal theory and research experience regarding poverty problems and their causal determinants. This is not to imply, however, as some have asserted, that there were no underlying theoretical persuasions surrounding the nature of antipoverty objectives. Peter Marris and Martin Rein in *Dilemmas of Social Reform* argue persuasively that an antipoverty "philosophy" did reside among many of the early antipoverty strategists.[5] There were several major ideas around which this philosophy coalesced:

> Poverty and delinquency were perpetuated by an inherited failure to respond, through ignorance, apathy and discouragement to the demands of urban civilization. The institutions of education and welfare had grown too insensitive and rigid to retrieve these failures, from a characteristic, morbid preoccupation with the maintenance of their organizational structure. The processes of assimilation were breaking down, and could only be repaired by an enlargement of opportunities. But this emancipation would only come about as the enabling institutions of assimilation—the schools, the welfare agencies, the vocational services—recognized their failure and became more imaginative, coherent and responsive. The attack was directed at a self-protective hardening of middle-class American society, which at once neglected and condemned those it excluded.[6]

It was from this perspective that the Gray Areas program and many of the activities of the President's Committee were launched. It was also this persuasion that heavily influenced the architects of the war on poverty.

Early antipoverty efforts conducted during this period were oriented largely toward interruption of a perceived "cycle of pov-

[4]Levitan, Sar A., "The Design of Antipoverty Strategy," in *Aspects of Poverty*, edited by Ben B. Seligman (New York: Thomas Crowell, 1968) p. 252.
[5]See Marris, Peter and Rein, Martin, *Dilemmas of Social Reform: Poverty and Community Action in the United States* (New York: Atherton Press, 1967).
[6]Ibid., p. 53.

erty." This entailed vocational training and educational support for youth, job development and placement programs, as well as the provision of legal aid and other community services. Perhaps the most far-reaching dimension of early antipoverty strategy, however, was the stress on organizational reforms designed to upgrade community action. The community action commitment was derived from the idea that one of the major causal components associated with the cycle of poverty is a deficiency in political activity, efficacy and legitimacy on the part of the poor. Given the limited institutional base from which initial antipoverty efforts were launched, it was perceived as imperative that the poor develop their own independent political base from which to enlarge and safeguard poverty programs.

Community action, during this period, entailed the creation of local organizations that enlisted citizen participation in the drafting and submission of grant proposals for antipoverty aid. Community involvement from these earliest planning stages was considered a major safeguard against contamination of poverty efforts by hostile bureaucratic interests.

It is not appropriate here to describe in detail the design and practice of these early antipoverty programs. But it *is* important to evaluate these formative efforts from the standpoint of those threshold problems in antipoverty objectives with which they were confronted. It is in this early stage of antipoverty policy development that inherent requisites of scale are well revealed.

Basically, three major deficiencies beset antipoverty efforts during this period: an absence of political activation on the part of the poor; vastly inadequate organizational resources; and a lack of coherence in program application. From these deficiencies a variety of secondary dilemmas followed in turn.

Problems of Political Quiescence. Antipoverty policy in its early stages entailed the design and pursuit of projects directed toward a clientele singularly devoid of political energy.[7] Perhaps no other factor was as crucial to the pursuit of poverty policy in this early period as this. The absence of political mobilization on the part of the poor led first to an indifference and, later, to unreserved hostility from established political and bureaucratic interests. The absence of a politically articulate constituency left the reform projects of the Ford Foundation and the President's Committee in precarious in-

[7]Economist Gunnar Myrdal has referred to America's poor as "the world's least revolutionary proletariat." See Myrdal, Gunnar, "The War on Poverty," in *New Perspectives on Poverty*, edited by Arthur B. Shostak and William Gomberg (Englewood Cliffs, NJ: Prentice-Hall, 1965) p. 122.

stitutional positions vis-à-vis these interests. This basic political insecurity was responsible for a multitude of specific problems in early antipoverty efforts.

One such problem involved the resistance of professional educators and school officials to provisions in many of the educational opportunity programs for the poor. These programs frequently sought to induce curricular and grading reforms, new teaching and counselling techniques, and even home visitation on the part of teachers.[8] Because of the novelty of these approaches, many educators were suspicious of their intent and resentful of perceived intrusions upon professional autonomy. Yet the lack of an institutional base from which to implement their programs forced early poverty officials to rely solely upon the cooperation of the schools—a requirement that necessitated delicate and complex negotiations, frequent delays and program compromises which led to highly uncertain implementation in the best of cases and subversion of intent in the worst.

Attempts at the selective mobilization of poverty clientele proved scarcely more successful. One such effort was made by the Mobilization for Youth project in New York City. Leaders of this project "recognized the limitations of cooperation, and used it [sic] to justify a more aggressive approach. Since Mobilization believed that the exercise of power would help the poor to overcome their apathy, it turned to the organization of pressure upon the schools."[9]

Yet the Mobilization project soon discovered itself to be in a position from which selective political pressure could not successfully be applied. The schools had the power to resist such pressure by employing a strategy termed by E. E. Schattschneider, the "socialization of conflict."[10] As Schattschneider asserts, "As likely as not, the audience determines the outcome of a fight."[11] By escalating the public scope of controversy, the schools were able to project their disputes with the Mobilization project into a political arena in which their resources were simply overwhelming. The schools, in other words, "could expose Mobilization to national attention. . . . Mobilization was not prepared to withstand an attack on this scale, and lacked a political constituency large enough to defend it."[12]

Here a major threshold problem is illustrated. The project was confronted with an *absence of middle ground* between total depen-

[8]Marris and Rein, op. cit., p. 59.
[9]Ibid., p. 67.
[10]See Schattschneider, E. E., *The Semi-Sovereign People* (New York: Holt, Rinehart and Winston, 1960).
[11]Ibid., p. 2.
[12]Marris and Rein, op. cit., p. 69.

dency upon school system cooperation (with its attendent threat of program distortion) and high level political conflict in which their limited constituency support was easily overwhelmed. "Mobilization for Youth found, then, that it could not pursue a militant strategy on its own terms, limiting the conflict to issues of its choosing. Any confrontation exposed it to the risk of an overwhelmingly virulent reaction, which it lacked the resources to withstand, while cooperation robbed it of the freedom to attempt any radical innovation."[13]

This dilemma encountered by the Mobilization project surrounded many of the other antipoverty programs of this period as well. With no activation on the part of the poor and no legitimate institutional base from which to gain policy compliance from established bureaucracies, the Grey Areas and President's Committee undertakings generally foundered. Most remained in inchoate and turbulent organizational states.

Problems in Resource Deficiency. A second major contributing factor to the effectiveness problems of these early antipoverty efforts was a deficiency in resources with which they were afflicted. The President's Committee appropriations ran from $6 to $8 million annually with less than $11 million available for project support in its first three years. The Ford Foundation, meanwhile, appropriated approximately $20 million all told to its Grey areas and related programs.[14] These funds were limited in both amount and application. Most of the President's Committee's resources, for example, were directed toward planning grants substantially detached from the establishment of frameworks for program implementation and action. The grey areas project channeled its funds into only five major cities and the state of North Carolina.

Limited funding and commensurately small staffing undermined seriously the effectiveness of these early antipoverty undertakings. Moreover, the projects were consistently unable to generate the commitment of public resources at the local level—resources which were urgently needed to augment their own inadequate funding. The indifference of local communities left the projects not only undersupported, but also fragmented and isolated, without coordination with existing urban programs. As Marris and Rein assert: "In the end, cities seldom made any substantial contributions from their own resources . . . , innovative ideas tended to relapse into conventional practice, or were simply ignored; undertakings were

[13]Idem.
[14]Levitan, op. cit., p. 253, and Marris and Rein, op. cit., pp. 28–29.

not honored; or programs which should have reinforced each other
were, for administrative convenience, implemented without coordination."[15]

Problems of Coordination and coherence. The coordination difficulties encountered in these early antipoverty programs are particularly significant insofar as thresholds in poverty objectives are concerned. As poverty-cycle theory asserted, the causal determinants of poverty were multiple and interrelated, requiring concerted attack on many fronts. Antipoverty policy architects were persuaded as to the necessity of this approach and entertained hopes that such a coordinated set of attacks could be designed. " 'We wanted to provide a framework,' as Lloyd Ohlin, consultant to the President's Committee, explained, 'where we could concentrate a whole series of programs together in the same area. This would show greater impact. We felt that the problem was not just one of providing new services here and there but of *trying to reach a new threshold* by an integrated approach [emphasis added].' "[16] It was just this aspiration that was not realized, indeed could not be realized, at the scale of these pioneering programs.

Many important aspects of the poverty "problems" addressed by these early efforts lay essentially outside the range of their possible impact. The job training and placement projects, for example, could only hope to be effective insofar as jobs were actually available in private sector industries and these industries were willing to hire the disadvantaged. The education projects depended upon the cooperation of educational bureaucracies which had few incentives and fewer guidelines under which to offer it. All of the poverty projects depended, in a larger sense, upon the performance of the American economy.

It was the growing realization of the need to gain some measure of control over many of these external poverty-influencing factors—the need for a concerted and comprehensive antipoverty approach—that was in large part responsible for the arousal of governmental interest in a war on poverty. One might, in fact, argue that it was the implicit recognition of scale requisites associated with antipoverty objectives that motivated governmental policy planners.[17] This recognition, heightened during the early days of the

---

[15]Marris and Rein, op. cit., p. 148.
[16]Ibid., p. 141.
[17]For a useful account of this formative period of the war on poverty, see James L. Sundquist, "Origins of the War on Poverty," in *On Fighting Poverty*, edited by James L. Sundquist (New York: Basic Books, 1969), pp. 3–33; and Levitan, Sar, *The Great Society's Poor Law* (Baltimore: Johns Hopkins Press, 1969).

Kennedy administration, became a primary drive behind the early design of the war on poverty. As one analyst described it:

> The Kennedy piecemeal programs, built on those of his predecessors, were reaching toward the substratum of the population in which all the problems were concentrated but somehow not making contact, not on a scale and with an impact that measured up to the bright promise of a new Frontier. The measures enacted, and those proposed, were dealing separately with such problems as slum housing, juvenile delinquency, unemployment, dependency and illiteracy but *they were separately inadequate* because they were striking only at some of the surface aspects of a bedrock problem, and that bedrock problem had to be identified and defined so that it could be attacked in a concerted, unified and innovative way.[18]

Related to this sense of inefficacy surrounding the evaluation of existing programs was a growing realization within the Kennedy administration that the "spillover" effects of technology and prosperity were in themselves insufficient to result in the eradication of poverty. Economic expansion, once presumed to be the best overall remedy for problems of poverty, came under increasingly critical scrutiny in the Kennedy administration insofar as its antipoverty powers were concerned. The Council of Economic Advisors, under the direction of Walter Heller, in May of 1963, communicated a report to the President, asserting a diminishing impact of economic growth upon the reduction of "poor" families (annual income below $3000) in the United States. The Council's analysis "showed that for the postwar period ending in the early 1960s economic growth had apparently become continuously less effective in reducing poverty, and that the incidence of poverty, although declining, was declining at an ever slower rate. . . ."[19]

President Kennedy, apparently persuaded by these arguments, directed the Council, the Budget Bureau and the Departments of Labor and Health, Education, and Welfare "to make the case for a major policy attack on poverty."[20]

The Design and Prosecution of the War on Poverty

It remained for President Lyndon B. Johnson to propose formally in 1964 the war on poverty program. The architects of this program, many of whom had participated in Grey Areas or President's Com-

---

[18]Sundquist, op. cit., p. 8.

[19]Kershaw, Joseph A., *Government Against Poverty* (Washington, DC: The Brookings Institution, 1970) p. 22.

[20]Plotnick, Robert D. and Skidmore, Felicity, *Progress Against Poverty* (New York: Academic Press, 1975) p. 3.

mittee projects, were sensitive to the scale dilemmas encountered in the earlier antipoverty efforts. Many scale requisites were directly addressed in the proposal to the Congress of the Economic Opportunity Act.

Recognition of the need for coordination and coherence in antipoverty programming, for example, was reflected in the proposed Office of Economic Opportunity—an independent agency within the Executive Office of the President, described as "a national headquarters for the war against poverty." In communicating the Economic Opportunity Act to Congress, President Johnson asserted that "I do not intend that the war against poverty become a series of uncoordinated and unrelated efforts—that it perish for lack of leadership and direction."[21]

Problems relating to political mobilization were attacked in the Economic Opportunity Act on two fronts. First, the Act proposed creation of the Community Action Program, designed to activate local citizens and the poor themselves (although in ways initially unspecified), on behalf of antipoverty programs. In addition, by asserting a Presidential commitment, the Johnson administration was in effect "nationalizing" the war—or, in Schattschneider's terms, enlarging the political arenas within which poverty programs could successfully compete.

Lastly, the antipoverty act addressed itself to the resource deficiencies encountered by earlier poverty efforts. President Johnson proposed the appropriation of $970 million to finance the war on poverty during fiscal year 1965 and called for the enlistment of thousands of antipoverty personnel.

Primarily, the EOA consisted of job training and education programs for youth, the Community Action Program, a volunteer project (VISTA), and rural and small business loans. With large Democratic majorities in both houses of Congress, the EOA was enacted substantially as President Johnson proposed it (with an $800 million appropriation for fiscal year 1965) after only a minimum legislative delay.

Policy Problems Relating to Scale. It is appropriate at this point to portray important contrasts between the prosecution of the war on poverty and the development of the space program in its postlegislative period. Although both undertakings had been launched under Presidential mandate and strong Congressional endorsement, dissimilarities between the two are evident at once.

The consolidation and integration of components of the two

[21]*Public Papers of the Presidents, Lyndon B. Johnson, 1963–64,* p. 379.

policies varied substantially. NASA, upon its formation, began to acquire control over major research and development projects of forseeable consequence to manned space exploration. In poverty policy, however, a very different consolidation pattern developed. The Office of Economic Opportunity was never able to gain an effective integration among the major offenses of the war on poverty. Of the programs outlined in the Opportunity Act, only Community Action, the Job Corps, Vista and the Migrant Farm Workers programs fell under the direct jursidiction of OEO. The Neighborhood Youth Corps was quickly placed under the management of the Department of Labor, the College Work Study and Work Experience programs fell to H.E.W., the Rural Loan and Small Business Development programs were delegated to the Department of Agriculture and Small Business Administration, respectively. These agencies were instructed to cooperate with the Director of OEO, and the delegated programs were financed through appropriations made to the Economic Opportunity Office, but in practice the coordination did not go smoothly. As one observer noted:

> [Throughout the history of the war on poverty] . . . the business of delegation has raised a number of questions. Not the least of these is who is responsible for a delegated program. It might seem clear that OEO's director should be responsible—it is his authorization by law and the funds are his by appropriation. But it is not that simple. While the director has to fit the delegated programs into the overall war against poverty, each agency administering a delegated program also has its own constituency to think of, and conflicts have never been far below the surface.[22]

Not only were there specific problems of coordination arising from the delegation of programs (and in this regard conflicts between OEO and the Department of Labor in connection with the Neighborhood Youth Corps were particularly acute) but the war on poverty as a policy lacked coherence on a much larger scale. The entire public assistance program of the Federal government and the Federal and state unemployment compensation program were unincorporated into the framework of the war. These programs addressed large numbers of constituents identified as "poor" (and consequently claimed by OEO) and at the same time commanded enormous financial resources. In fiscal year 1965, the first year of OEO operation, Federal outlays for major public assistance programs alone amounted to $3.7 billion and these funds reached over 7 mil-

[22]Kershaw, *Government Against Poverty*, op. cit., pp. 152–153.

lion recipients.[23] (Contrast this with OEO's appropriation for 1965 of $800 million.) These public assistance and unemployment compensation programs amounted to substantial interventions in the "poverty constituency" yet they were ungovernable in connection with antipoverty policy. Moreover, during the life of the war these programs were to grow and diversify at impressive rates, with public assistance expenditures (including newer medicare, medicaid and food stamp outlays) amounting to over $27 billion by 1973.[24] In the detachment of these programs from the framework of the war on poverty, a major source of problem-solving leverage was denied to poverty policy makers.

In short, the design of the war did not feature an administrative and programmatic cohesion at anywhere near the level attained in the space program. In fact, one antipoverty policy analyst has contended that "It is apparent from the legislative history of the Economic Opportunity Act that no overall rational plan dictated either the selection of programs to be included in the Act or their distribution between the new OEO and federal agencies already in the poverty business."[25]

A second important departure between the war and space program can be found in the rate of increase in budgetary allocations accorded to each. It is inappropriate to compare actual allocations to the two policies directly, as if poverty and space "dollars" were equivalent units, but it *is* useful to consider in each case the relationship between expenditures prior to policy acceleration (as a base) and subsequent appropriations after Presidential commitment. It is also revealing to relate postcommitment expenditures to the *expectations* of support residing among policy makers themselves.

First, a brief reminiscence regarding space program growth. Table 5-1 displays rates of appropriations increase for NASA over each previous fiscal year during the period 1960–1966.

As can readily be discerned, the expansion of appropriations to the space program was very rapid—representing an immediate and sizeable series of dollar increases over those expenditures made prior to policy acceleration. Even before the lunar landing commitment, the formation of NASA itself in 1958 led to a 62 percent increase in

[23]These figures include expenditures under the Aid to the Aged, Blind and Disabled as well as the Aid to Families with Dependent Children programs. See Schultze, Charles L. et al., *Setting National Priorities: The 1973 Budget* (Washington, DC: The Brookings Institution, 1972) p. 188.

[24]See Blechman, Barry M. et al., *Setting National Priorities: The 1975 Budget* (Washington, DC: The Brookings Institution, 1974) p. 168.

[25]Levitan, Sar A. and Davidson, Roger H., *Anti-Poverty Housekeeping: The Administration of the Economic Opportunity Act* (Ann Arbor: University of Michigan Press, 1968) p. 6.

Table 5.1. Rates of Appropriation Increase—NASA (FY 1960-66)[a]

Fiscal Year	Rate of Increase[b]
1960	58.4
1961	84.7
1962	88.9
1963	101.3
1964	38.8
1965	2.9
1966	1.4

[a]Compiled from data obtained from NASA, Program and Special Reports Division, Washington, D.C.
[b]Percentage of gain over previous fiscal year.

research and development and research plant expenditures in the very next year.[26]

The war on poverty, despite its rhetorical presentation, experienced only a marginal build-up and expansion, particularly in relation to total expenditures for public assistance-oriented programs. Table 5-2 depicts OEO and antipoverty related expenditures during the 1965–1974 period. In addition, it displays the rates of increase in these funds during each fiscal year. No rate of increase is computed for FY 1966 as the 1965 appropriation was for a six-month period only. FY 1966 is the first full-year OEO appropriation.

Table 5.2. OEO and Antipoverty-Related Expenditures: FY1965–74[a]

Fiscal Year	Expenditures ($ × 10⁶)	%-age Increase Over Previous Fiscal Year
1965	737.0	——
1966	1403.6	——[b]
1967	1623.4	15
1968	1695.5	4
1969	1896.1	11
1970	1824.9	-3
1971	1285.5	-29
1972	681.2	-47
1973	465.4	-31
1974	328.5	-29

[a]Compiled from Plotnick, Robert and Skidmore, Felicity, *Progress Against Poverty* (New York: Academic Press, 1975) pp. 8–10.
[b]No percentage computed due to half-year appropriation in FY 1965.

---

[26]See, for data regarding research expenditures over time, *Federal Funds for Research and Development and Other Scientific Activities*, National Science Foundation (Washington, DC: U.S. Government Printing Office, 1970) pp. 230–231.

Also revealing are comparisons between poverty program funds and amounts spent on low income and public assistance support. These latter funds represent, in some respects, the "unincorporated resources" denied to the war on poverty: their proportion provides a sense of scale regarding poverty program expenditures. (See Table 5-3.)

As is suggested here, the resource scales of the war on poverty and space program varied considerably. The war was never funded at levels anticipated in line with its publicly asserted tasks nor was it able to gain any measure of incorporation or control over those programs that were accorded large appropriations and that directed them toward appropriate constituencies. Manned space exploration, in contrast, featured a coordinating agency (NASA) that gained jurisdiction over the majority of funds spent within a sustained period on space exploration research and hardware development. In fact, during its appropriations peak in 1966, NASA expenditures accounted for almost 37 percent of *all* research and development and R&D-plant funds spent throughout the entire Federal government.[27]

As is evident, the war on poverty was placed within an appropriations framework far different from that experienced by NASA. OEO was never able to attain the level of support required to mount an effective attack upon those thresholds associated with poverty policy making. "Basic to all other problems [was] the lack of resources to do the job."[28]

Moreover, the rate of OEO's appropriations increase was never matched appropriately with poverty policy *expectations*. The promise of continuing and enlarging support, so important in the early stages of the space program, was significantly eroded within the

Table 5.3. OEO and Antipoverty Expenditures vs. Federal Low-Income and Public Assistance Expenditures[a] (Selected Fiscal Years)

Fiscal Year	OEO and Antipoverty Expenditures[b]	Low-income and Public Assistance[b]	% OEO vs, L.I.–P.A.
1970	1824.9	12,927	14
1973	465.4	20,945	2

[a]Includes unemployment compensation, AFDC, Food stamp, Medicaid programs, etc., *excludes* social security, medicare and other retirement expenditures.
[b]In millions of dollars.

[27]Idem.
[28]Kershaw, op. cit., p. 165.

framework of poverty program finance. At the outset of the war, expectations were high that a substantial enlargement of funds would take place in subsequent years—expectations held among policy makers and policy recipients alike. Yet clearly such increases did not occur. "Instead of expanding antipoverty programs, OEO in 1967 was fighting for its very life."[29] Important problems of management as well as substantial political turbulence were introduced into the poverty program because of its funding insecurities. As two poverty analysts contend:

> Of all OEO travails, those associated with funding were the most serious impediment to efficient and smooth operations. That there was not enough money to wage 'an unconditional war on poverty' needs no repetition; but the way Congress handled the annual OEO appropriations bears particular emphasis. . . . Even within the usual constraints of annual budgeting, Congress seemed to do its utmost to prevent orderly planning and administration of EOA efforts.[30]

Under these financial circumstances, many long-range planning efforts undertaken within the poverty agency had to be abandoned. In addition, operating programs of the war also suffered considerably. Community action was one such program in particular.

> The growth and development of community action was stunted after its first year when, in December 1965, the White House imposed severe and unexpected budgetary limitations on domestic programs for the period beginning July 1, 1966. These limitations were made more severe the next year when Congress earmarked large portions of community action funds for specific programs. This double deceleration of the community action program was particularly painful because of disappointed expectations around the country, right down to the neighborhood level in city after city. The limitations also made it harder to recruit and retain capable local administrators and project directors, whose presence may turn out to be the single most important variable in the success of local programs.[31]

Budgetary stringency during the critical developmental period of the war not only undermined the evolution of poverty programs, it also placed these programs within much more turbulent political environments. "OEO found that it had created activities and expectations in more communities than it was able to persuade the Congress to finance during succeeding years, so that incipient programs

[29]Levitan and Davidson, op. cit., p. 27.
[30]Ibid., p. 58.
[31]Wofford, John G., "The Politics of Local Responsibility: Administration of the Community Action Program," in *On Fighting Poverty*, edited by James L. Sundquist, p. 101.

were not funded and existing programs sometimes cut back."[32] The
cutback of these programs aroused cynicism and antagonism toward
OEO on the part of many of those who had become self-identified as
war on poverty clientele. For many poverty projects, there was "little difficulty in evoking a response from the people they tried to
serve: their most urgent and intractable problem was to satisfy the
demand they raised."[33] Ultimately, some have contended, unful-
filled antipoverty expectations contributed to outbreaks of urban
violence throughout the United States in the middle and late 1960s.
In this connection, Detroit Mayor Jerome Cavanagh asserted after
the July 1967 riots in his city: "What we've been doing, at the level
we've been doing it, is almost worse than nothing at all. . . . We've
raised expectations, but we haven't been able to deliver all we
should have. . . ."[34]

Additional Poverty Program Deficiencies. Administrative consolidation and budgetary support are not the only points of departure
between the space program and the war on poverty. The prosecution
of the war never attained the degree of political independence and
self-sufficiency evidenced by space exploration after the Kennedy
lunar landing commitment. I have discussed earlier the importance
to large-scale policy objectives of such independence. These objectives in their pursuit are highly vulnerable to the reduction and
compromise processes associated with conventional political
negotiation. Such processes are forces of disaggregation which
threaten to push large-scale undertakings below one or more critical
effectiveness thresholds.

In the case of antipoverty policy, a self-sustaining political foundation did not ensue from the Johnson mandate to end poverty. It is,
in fact, very revealing to note how quickly the Johnson mandate
itself eroded under the impact of political attack. As poverty programs began to confront established political interests and arouse
new political activism among heretofore quiescent clienteles, a
presidential retrenchment began. "Less was heard of the 'War on
Poverty' and more of the 'poverty program.' And the latter had a
much narrower definition. . . ."[35] A Lyndon Johnson increasingly
preoccupied with the conduct of another war—the war in
Vietnam—had little interest in further association with a policy
beset on all sides by political controversy.

For the poverty program, the Johnson mandate was in no sense

[32]Yarmolinsky, Adam, "The Beginnings of OEO," in Sundquist, op. cit., p. 50.
[33]Marris and Rein, op. cit., p. 225.
[34]Cavanagh, Jerome P., as quoted in Kershaw, op. cit., p. 166.
[35]Sundquist, op. cit., p. 31.

the mobilizing and sustaining force that the Kennedy commitment proved to be in the case of manned space exploration. Indeed, "few would have dared predict on the midday in January 1964 when a new President declared 'unconditional war on poverty,' saying that the objective was 'total victory,' that in the months ahead the presidential resolve would diminish and withdraw, not all at once, but in numerous, painful, almost measureless ways."[36]

The consequences of this diminishing resolve were widely ramified throughout the poverty program. A direct effect was the increased vulnerability of the war on poverty to external intrusion and intervention. The Economic Opportunity Act itself was subject to frequent Congressional amendment—altering the foundation upon which the war depended. Particularly vulnerable to legislative modification was the Community Action Program. Political turmoil engulfed community action projects at their outset with disputes centering around representation of the poor, the selection of objectives and the political independence of the projects from City Hall jurisdictions.[37] As a result of these antagonisms, important revisions were made in the operating guidelines of the community action program.

One such modification resulted from the well-publicized "Green amendment" to the Opportunity Act. This 1967 reform enabled city administrations "to assume sponsorship of Community Action Programs."[38] The Green amendment, coupled with internal executive directives from the Bureau of the Budget to OEO officials, placed community action more squarely within conventional urban institutional settings than antipoverty architects had originally intended. In addition, an earlier legislative action had an even more direct effect in undermining the independence of the community action program. In 1966, under pressure from many of the nation's mayors, Congress enacted the Model Cities program. This represented an alternative and competing approach to urban housing and antipoverty policy making. Termed a "mayor's program," model cities was directed at many of those same problems addressed by community action but was firmly under the control of local governments. Moreover, model cities by virtue of its administrative location within the department of Housing and Urban Development represented yet another set of antipoverty resources detached from OEO jurisdiction and the framework of the war.

[36]Selover, William C., "The View From Capitol Hill: Harrassment and Survival," in *On Fighting Poverty*, edited by James L. Sundquist, p. 185.

[37]For an interesting treatment of the controversy surrounding the Community Action Program, see Moynihan, Daniel P., *Maximum Feasible Misunderstanding* (New York: The Free Press, 1969).

[38]Plotnick and Skidmore, *Progress Against Poverty*, op. cit., p. 24.

The Poverty War and the Welfare Establishment. Perhaps the most revealing illustration of the failure of the war on poverty to gain the degree of political self-sufficiency acquired by the space program is the "capture" of many antipoverty undertakings by established welfare personnel and institutions. One of the viewpoints, it will be recalled, taken to heart by many antipoverty policy architects was that professionalized bureaucracies in welfare and education had lost both the sensitivity and flexibility to deal effectively with problems of the poor.

> OEO was at first conceived as independent of the "welfare professionals" who had traditionally dealt with the needy and the unskilled—educators, training specialists and social workers. However well-intentioned the traditional welfare programs had been, Shriver and many of his associates seemed to believe that they had stagnated in the hands of the professional associations and state agencies which controlled them. Moreover, these groups were accused of having 'captured' some bureaus in the Department of Health, Education and Welfare which were charged with implementing national programs.[39]

Early antagonisms erupted between these "welfare professionals" and poverty program officials as the latter attempted to assert and maintain their independence. Yet, ultimately, without adequate resources or a self-sustaining political base, major compromises had to be made in the conduct of the war to the power of established welfare interests. In its precarious political position, "OEO could not live without the welfare profession and ... it soon realized this fact."[40]

Unlike the pursuit of space exploration, the war on poverty was never able to attain an organizational transcendence of those limiting factors associated with conventional policy compromise and competition. Yet these very limiting factors were perceived by many antipoverty policy makers to be *precisely at the heart of the poverty problem.* "Whether OEO liked it or not, existing organizational and personnel resources were firmly in the hands of the so-called professionals. Of necessity, OEO found many of its dollars going to the same interests which had been administering the traditional programs."[41]

The final set of jurisdictional battles lost by OEO were fought over control of its original set of core programs, and ultimately, over the agency's survival itself. Between 1965 and 1969, OEO lost no fewer than eight of its programs to rival cabinet departments and executive agencies. Some of the initial losses were major ones—

[39]Davidson and Levitan, op. cit., p. 45.
[40]Ibid., p. 46.
[41]Ibid., pp. 45–46.

Work Study, Adult Education, Head Start and Upward Bound programs transferred to H.E.W.; the Neighborhood Youth Corps and Job Corps to the Department of Labor.[42] The dissolution accelerated between 1971 and 1974, and in the latter year OEO itself was abolished by Congress, the war on poverty having long since been abandoned as a viable policy by the executive branch.

Antipoverty Policy: Performance and Factors of Scale

The inventory presented here of policy problems associated with the war on poverty is clearly not an evaluation of the *effects* of the war on the dimensions of American poverty. Such evaluations have proven extremely difficult despite intensive political and academic interest in them—just as evaluation has proven difficult in a variety of other policy areas.[43]

Statistical analyses reveal a significant drop in the number of American families living below "official" poverty income levels during the 1965–1968 period.[44] But beyond this evidence, assessments of the war are contradictory. There are no persuasively demonstrated causal linkages, for example, between this statistical decline and the war on poverty specifically. Many other public welfare-oriented programs were in operation during this same period. Moreover, two antipoverty analysts have contended in this connection that "the most effective antipoverty program of the 1960s was the Vietnam war."[45] (Also at issue in the evaluation of the poverty program is the contention that the number of families living in relative poverty has actually *increased* since 1968.)[46]

For our purposes here, however, certain assessments of the war on poverty can be safely undertaken aside from these controversies. Clearly, the war has failed in its publicly stated objective of "total victory" in the elimination of American poverty. It has failed to live up to those expectations it aroused among its own clientele. The

[42]For an account of this jurisdictional decay see James, Dorothy B., *Analyzing Poverty Policy* (Lexington, MA: Lexington Books, 1975).

[43]For a discussion of evaluation difficulties connected with the war, see Rossi, Peter, "Practice, Method and Theory in Evaluating Social Action Programs," in Sundquist, op. cit., pp. 217–234; and Williams, Walter and Evans, John W., The politics of evaluation: The case of head start, *Annals of the American Academy of Political and Social Science* 385 (September, 1969): 118–132.

[44]See Blechman, Barry M., et al., *Setting National Priorities: The 1975 Budget*, op. cit., p. 167; and Plotnick and Skidmore, op. cit., pp. 169–189. For a more general assertion of success regarding the war and other "Great Society" programs see Levitan, Sar and Taggart, Robert, *The Promise of Greatness* (Cambridge: Harvard University Press, 1976).

[45]Levitan, Sar and Mangum, Garth, Programs and priorities, *The Reporter* (September 7, 1967) p. 22.

[46]Plotnick and Skidmore, op. cit., p. 175.

war has also failed to sustain itself as an ongoing public policy ven- ture as the elimination of many of its programs and the dissolution of OEO well attest.

Yet for all this, there is a failure associated with the war on poverty that is even more important from our standpoint. This is the failure of the poverty program in its operation and institutionalization *to reflect the theories and design of its architects.* Here, indeed, is the failure of a policy—large-scale in its objectives and design—to find accommodation in an appropriate political and organizational environment.

Antipoverty policy, in the eyes of its primary theoreticians and managers, was an enterprise with important requisites associated with its pursuit. Among these requisites were a political activation on the part of the poor; a substantial commitment of public resources for education and employment programs; and a detachment of these programs from unresponsive and self-serving welfare bureaucracies. As it turned out, these proved to be large-scale requisites; that is, they had to be provided at high levels or they simply could not be provided at all. Antipoverty policy requisites could not be attained in piecemeal fashion appropriate to conventional pluralist processes. Instead, they were beset by thresholds just as were those requisites associated with manned space exploration. In this case, however, these thresholds were never breached in the institutional expression of the policy.

Consider the resources allocated to the war. OEO appropriations, it is generally acknowledged, were never remotely adequate to the public challenges that were set for it. Major public welfare funds, at the same time, remained unincorporated into the war. Institutionalization of the war at relatively low resource scales precluded the ultimate attainment of adequate appropriations requirements. Such institutionalization occurred at a very early stage of the poverty program because of the failure of the Johnson administration to push *at the outset* for rapid expansion.

These resource problems reflect, in fact, an *appropriations growth threshold* upon which antipoverty policy foundered. Expansion had to come swiftly and in large scale if it was to occur in any significant measure. Otherwise the policy became "locked-in" to a political and psychological framework that precluded major growth. As one poverty analyst contended:

One danger of a continuation of budgets . . . is that *they tend to become institutionalized in people's minds.* When appropriations have been between $1.5 and $2 billion for four or five years, there is an inclination to think of $2.5 billion as a substantial increase. The fact is that there is no real difference between $2 and $2.5 billion; neither one will make an impact upon the problem we confront. What is called for is a tripling, or more, not small increments, and as each year passes with budget levels remaining essentially constant, this becomes more difficult to achieve, and spokesmen for the program become more reluctant to press for significant changes—they fear they will not be taken seriously.[47]

In the meantime, without major appropriations growth, the poverty program became exceedingly vulnerable to Congressional attack and ultimate budgetary reductions. It had failed to reach a critical "capture point" of public investment.

> Had OEO programs been given the opportunity to expand in 1965, it is not likely that Congress would have cut existing programs during the subsequent two years. It is easier to prevent expansion of programs than to retrench ongoing efforts. Reduction of the OEO budget would have meant loss of jobs in communities and elimination of services. Few Congressmen would take such a step lightly.[48]

Unable to breach the appropriations growth threshold, the war on poverty was left seriously deficient in resources required to do its job. These deficiencies, moreover, translated themselves into the adoption of program strategies that, in turn, failed to provide secondary policy requirements. Funds were allocated thinly over many geographical areas rather than concentrated in a select number of high density poverty areas where they might have yielded a greater impact. This strategy, while designed to maximize political support, lowered significantly the distribution of resources per poor person in relation to what could otherwise have been obtained. As a result, "almost everywhere the resources [were] too small to show impact."[49]

Political Activation Dilemmas. The political arousal of poverty clientele proved to be another policy factor inflexible in scale. Political activation of the poor did not seem to come in intermediate and continuous quantities. Instead, the poverty program confronted at its outset apathetic and politically disaffected clientele— unorganized and unskilled in the presentation of demands in pluralist arenas. Then, once in operation, the program faced an opposite condition. The establishment of the war dramatically raised

---

[47]Kershaw, op. cit., p. 166.

[48]Davidson and Levitan, op. cit., p. 61. Anthony Downs asserts that precisely this growth and dependency threshold must be attained, and attained quickly, if bureaucratic organizations in general are to survive. See *Inside Bureaucracy* (Boston: Little, Brown, 1967) Chapter 2.

[49]Kershaw, p. 64.

expectations on the part of many poverty clients. These expectations led to a previously unencountered militancy in their press for
reform, while at the same time contributing to disillusionment and
subsequent hostility when such reform was not swiftly forthcoming. This escalation of expectations among poverty clientele is not,
of course, dissimilar from that historically observed in association
with social revolution or reform.[50] But, for the war, it proved to be
an occurrence with distinctly troublesome implications.

For the war on poverty, political activation on the part of the poor
was a policy component ill-suited to the political framework within
which the war had been cast. Militant expectations for reform
clashed sharply with the precarious compromise, bargaining and
coalition-building environment within which the poverty program
was forced to operate. Moreover, this activation of the poor aroused
a countermobilization on the part of those established urban interests who perceived themselves threatened by the emergence of a
rival and militant political constituency.

> Articulate and activist representatives of the poor are bound to clash
> with merchants, landlords, welfare officials and politicians. In many
> communities, northern as well as southern, OEO's clienteles
> threatened to grow into "anti-establishment" political groups. Local
> political leaders transmitted their concerns to their congressmen who,
> especially within the Democratic party, were sensitive to challenges
> to the party's big-city base of power.[51]

In the midst of this activation and counteractivation:

> OEO found itself pulled in opposite directions. On the one hand, in-
> creasingly militant reformers were demanding a radical shake-up of
> existing political and social service practices. On the other hand, es-
> tablished political groups were alternatively responsive and hostile.
> The more members of disadvantaged groups who were brought to the
> threshold of participation, the greater the potential impact upon es-
> tablished leaders. To the extent that OEO insisted on, for example,
> "maximum feasible participation" or racial integration in its pro-
> grams, it encountered hostility from City Hall and Congress. To the
> extent that it yielded to political realities and compromises, it faced
> rejection by the militants. *On a thousand different battlegrounds,*
> *OEO found itself in an unenviable stance in the middle* [emphasis
> added].[52]

---

[50]See, in this regard, James C. Davies' classic statement, Toward a theory of revolution, *Ameri-can Sociological Review*, 27(1) (February, 1962): 5–19.
[51]Davidson and Levitan, op. cit., pp. 71–72.
[52]Ibid., pp. 73–74.

It was in a larger sense this very stance "in the middle" that proved the undoing of the war on poverty. Because *it was precisely here—in the middle—that the major requisites of poverty policy could not be secured.* It was at the middle levels of politics—in the pluralist arena—that the war on poverty was singularly disadvantaged. The activation of its clientele did not come in quantities appropriate to this level. The growth rate and scale of appropriated funds was insufficient at this political location. The "capture point" that was required in order to attain long-term political commitment to the war did not inhere at this level. Finally, the institutional self-sufficiency and administrative coherence required for a concerted attack on poverty simply could not be obtained in the pluralist political arena—an arena of fragmentation and competitive jurisdictional intrusions.

Here, in short, is the classic problem confronting large-scale policy. The war on poverty was beset by thresholds in those policy components perceived essential to its pursuit. These thresholds, and the indivisibility they infused into the design of the war, could not be successfully accommodated on the intermediate scale and in the disaggregated and divisible framework within which it was cast. As a result, the conduct of the war was never appropriately matched to the design of its architects.

It is important to understand the thrust and implications of this argument. It is *not* an argument that the war on poverty, if pursued on an appropriate scale, would have realized its end of "total victory" over American poverty. In this sense, no assessment is offered here of the wisdom contained in antipoverty theory. Instead, the argument is that the design of the war that reflected this theory was a *large-scale design*—that is, it established as requisites of antipoverty policy making political and organizational components to which thresholds were attached. The design of the war thus demanded conditions *which could not be realized* given implementation in a pluralist framework.

It is within this context that we have related mismatches in scale to performance problems associated with the poverty program. That the war failed to eradicate poverty in line with its stated objectives is not primarily at issue. What is decidedly at issue is the failure of the war to realize administratively its own design—*to put its program into practice.* Whether this program would have had, in fact, dramatic success in the eradication of poverty is a complex and currently unanswerable question. The contention here, however, is that because of scale mismatches, antipoverty policy was never given in effect a "fighting chance."

The War on Poverty and the Concept of Pluralism

It seems appropriate in concluding this discussion of problems of scale associated with the war on poverty to refer directly to the pluralist theory of the policy process. This theory asserts at once the existence of a multiplicity of interests in industrialized society; the ability of these interests to articulate themselves in groups; and the subsequent ability of groups to dominate the policy-making process through competitive interaction.[53] Pluralist theory stresses the likelihood of political interests to realize discrete policy benefits in proportion to their group activity and skill in the presentation of demands. It assumes that public policy outcomes will reflect specialized interest payoffs pieced together in flexible combination.

Yet this treatment of the war on poverty suggests a problem in pluralist theory. It reveals an exception to the process of multiple interest accommodation. The poverty program suggests that (1) some interests are unlikely to derive significant social benefits by means of the competitive arena if left to their own skills and resources; (2) that these interests require *government policy support* if they are to acquire competitive skills and resources, and (3) that such policy support may entail design and feasibility requirements *unfulfillable in this same competitive arena.*

The theory of pluralism, in other words, fails to allow at the outset for the dependency of an interest for political benefit upon large-scale policy. The theory then fails to treat the vulnerability of such policy to pursuit in competitive and pluralist settings.[54]

Without adequate education and income, and with little sense of political efficacy, the poor are systematically disadvantaged in the pluralist competition for social benefits. Yet the provision of these competitive resources may require policy measures which must transcend the very arena for which the poor are to be prepared. Without such transcendence the political weakness of the poor cannot sustain and support remedial policy efforts on their own behalf.

Thus, for certain interests, and the policies which support them, the pluralist arena is *not* an instrumentality leading to desired political outcomes. For the poor, political activation brought a "crushing

---

[53]For classic descriptions of pluralist theory see Truman, David B., *The Governmental Process* (New York: Alfred A. Knopf, 1951) and Dahl, Robert A., *Pluralist Democracy in the United States* (Chicago: Rand McNally, 1967). A more recent statement is Kelso, William A., *American Democratic Theory: Pluralism and Its Critics* (Westport, CN: Greenwood Press, 1978).

[54]For a discussion of other problems in the theory of pluralism see Smith, Michael P., *Politics in America* (New York: Random House, 1974) pp. 3-30.

revenge" from established interests in this arena.[55] For the poverty war in general, the policy components upon which its prosecution depended were not available for use in this arena.

These problems reflect the classic policy scale dilemma: without being large enough to breach thresholds of resource commitment and political independence, the war on poverty was *suddenly too large* for the protective power of its poverty clientele. This is a dilemma unrecognized and unaccountable by pluralist theory. Yet it was only too real for the clients and participants in the war on poverty.

[55]Sundquist, op. cit., p. 23.

Large-Scale Politics
and the War on Cancer

If the war on poverty illustrates those dilemmas that can confront policy objectives large-scale in implication when conducted within a competitive and disaggregated political framework, the more recent "war on cancer" illustrates the opposite problem. The attack on cancer represents a policy objective in all probability small-scale in its basic nature, yet currently cast within a large-scale organizational and political framework. This, too, is a mismatch with decidedly troublesome implications.

The Health Research Policy Culture

In analyzing those policy efforts undertaken under the rubric of the war on cancer, it is important to recognize at the outset a distinctive political and psychological environment that surrounds biomedical research. For this purpose it must be stated (and remembered) that policy pertaining to medical *research* displays a political pattern quite different from that of medical training or health care delivery. These latter efforts reflect conventional interest group pluralism in operation. Biomedical research, on the other hand, has been conducted within a policy pattern highly unusual among public undertakings.

Biomedical research is an example of Congressional policy making. It is the Congress that has consistently asserted public purpose with respect to this research, that has set specific research targets and priorities, and that has determined appropriate levels of public funding—frequently to the point of committing more funds to the enterprise than those requested by the executive branch and the research agencies themselves. Eluding both bureaucratic governance and, at times, Presidential attempts at control, biomedical research has emerged truly and unusually as a "Congressional program."[1]

This degree of Congressional dominance seems especially surprising in a policy area as technically arcane as biomedical research. One might well expect bureaucratic organizations within the executive branch to predominate given their traditional supremacy in the design and management of expertise-dependent activities. Moreover, biomedical researchers themselves might be expected to contribute to the isolation of research policy from Congressional intervention—doing so by demands for professional and scientific autonomy. Such has not been the case, however.

One important reason for the uniquely active Congressional role in biomedical research policy lies in a peculiar and widespread psychological orientation to such research—an emotional receptiveness that transcends many lines of political cleavage. Biomedical research is literally a "life and death" undertaking. It represents an attack upon those "dread diseases" (cancer, heart attack, stroke, and even aging) to which everyone, irrespective of their social or economic position, is subject. In the face of great personal insecurity regarding these diseases, it is psychologically reassuring to believe that everything that can be done to lessen their long-run threat is *currently being done.* "Medical research has enjoyed long popularity because it has been perceived as a weapon against a threat that is at once personal and national: dread disease."[2]

This psychology is highly significant as it provides a personalized foundation for collective political support of medical research efforts. Indeed, opinion surveys have consistently revealed extensive and sustained public approval for large expenditures in the health research area.[3]

[1]See Strickland, Stephen P., *Politics, Science and Dread Disease: A Short History of United States Medical Research Policy* (Cambridge: Harvard University Press, 1972) p. 94.

[2]Ibid., p. 257.

[3]On the average, approximately 80 percent of those surveyed over a 35-year period have consistently favored increases in cancer and heart disease research funds. A majority favor such increases even if taxes must be raised to pay for them. See Gallup, George H., *The Gallup Opinion Poll: Public Opinion, 1935–1971* (New York: Random House, 1972) pp. 583, 741, 1231 and 1248.

In addition to its predominance among the public, the health
research psychology also extends to congressmen themselves, functioning to mobilize their policy support. As one analyst explains it:

> Congressmen and Senators who live in spacious suburbs and send
> their children to excellent schools may be badly equipped to recognize
> the welfare needs of . . . less fortunate citizens. But they all know
> about cancer, fear retardation in their children, and have friends
> whose lives heart attacks have brought to an abrupt end.[4]

The psychology attached to health research has in no small way
contributed to its unique position among public policy ventures.
Congressmen have perceived that their enthusiasm for such research is a means to the development of broad constituency support. At the same time, the disease psychology provides real sanctions for negative behaviors regarding the promotion of research.
Few congressmen or political interests have been willing to risk the
public appearance of indifference or hostility to the humanitarian
attack on dread disease. "In practical terms, this . . . means that no
powerful lobbies stand, swords drawn, willing to slash away at the
medical research budget."[5]

In addition to this psychological component in the policy culture
surrounding biomedical research, there are important political factors that have enhanced the policy as well. One political advantage,
curiously enough, has been the consistent hostility of the American
Medical Association to efforts by the Congress to intervene in medical delivery and education practices in the United States. (It is appropriate to mention again that the policy characteristics to which
we have alluded in the area of health research emphatically do *not*
apply to health care delivery and training.) Here, the AMA, a powerful political force, has lobbied forcefully and successfully for nonintervention by Congress or other public institutions in the practice of
medicine. If health research has been the subject of lavish Congressional attention, health care has been jealously guarded by the AMA
as a *private* policy—subject appropriately only to self-regulation by
physicians' associations and medical school confederations.

The AMA has lobbied successfully against many forms of governmental health participation including third-party payments to
physicians (losing ultimately, after repeated opposition, to the Medicare and Medicaid insurance programs) and even federal support for
medical school construction and maintenance.[6] So adamant, in fact,

[4]Milton Viorst, The political good fortune of medical research, *Science* 144 (3616) (April 17, 1964): 267–268.

[5]Ibid., p. 268.

[6]For an account of AMA health care lobbying efforts, see Garceau, Oliver, *The Political Life of the American Medical Association* (Hamden, CN: Archon Books, 1961) and Ryack, Elton, *Professional Power and American Medicine* (Baltimore: Johns Hopkins Press, 1963).

have the AMA's lobbying efforts been in the area of health care delivery that the association has had neither the resources nor the inclination to participate in decisions involving health research undertakings. (It was only in 1964 that the AMA created a Commission on Research to review medical research activities conducted under federal sponsorship.)

This preoccupation of the AMA with health delivery issues not only left biomedical research policy relatively free from hostile scrutiny, it also made such policy highly attractive to these congressmen frustrated by AMA supremacy in other health areas.

> The AMA was so busy combating "socialized medicine" that it failed to notice the implications for medical practice and medical education of the growing federal budget for health research. This, in turn, provided health research as a platform from which congressmen could voice a concern for health without incurring the powerful wrath of the AMA.[7]

A second, and perhaps more important, political factor contributing to the unusual support surrounding health research policy has been a highly effective group of citizen lobbyists and sponsors. For over two decades, the most important member of this group was Mary Lasker, a wealthy New York health crusader who displayed impressive abilities to enlist important allies—the American Cancer Society, world-renowned medical researchers and physicians, influential journalists, and key congressmen and senators—in her cause. At the height of her power, one observer noted that "Mrs. Lasker's network is probably unparalleled in the influence that a small group of private citizens has had over such a major area of national policy."[8]

The health research lobby has effectively dominated through the Congress the targeting of federal research attacks on disease since the end of World War II. It has protected the jurisdiction and enlarged the appropriations of the National Institutes of Health as the country's primary biomedical research agency. In conjunction with chairmen of the House and Senate health appropriation subcommittees, the health lobby has formed a well-defined policy elite that has shielded biomedical research from much of the political fragmentation which characterizes conventional policies. For much of its history, "neither presidents, nor their cabinet secretaries in charge of health, nor their special offices for coordinating science policy could effectively control the direction or the pace of the federal biomedical

[7]Drew, Elizabeth, The health syndicate, *Atlantic Monthly* 220 (6) December, 1967):77
[8]Ibid., p. 76.

research effort."[9] This pattern of policy control is, again, highly unusual among public undertakings. It has had an important influence on the development and prosecution of the war on cancer.

Origins of the Cancer Crusade

The roots of government involvement in the fight against cancer are deeply set. As early as 1922, small research efforts directed at cancer were being conducted under sponsorship of the Public Health Service. Congressional attention to the cancer problem was first shown in 1927 when West Virginia Senator Matthew M. Neely introduced legislation to offer a reward of $5 million "to the first person who discovered a practical and successful cure for cancer."[10] Although Neely's proposal failed to gain Senate approval, interest in increased federal involvement in the fight against disease was expanding rapidly. In 1930 Congress passed the Ransdell Act creating a National Institute of Health in the Public Health Service to investigate causes and cures for a variety of human diseases, cancer among them. Interest in cancer research in particular continued to build and in 1937 Congress created a National Cancer Institute, although limiting its appropriations to $700,000 annually. Despite Public Health Service objections, a National Cancer Advisory Council was also established in that year to review all research projects undertaken by the new institute.

The creation of the National Cancer Institute was, in effect, the beginning of a series of categorical disease institutes that would ultimately come to comprise NIH. The disease-related names of the national health institutes well illustrate the politics surrounding biomedical research. Despite the preference of many scientists for institutes titled after disciplinary approaches to research, the increased political salience of names symbolizing attack on specific diseases has taken precedence. As described in one account:

> In the days when one of the NIH branches was called the Institute of Microbiology, one congressman asked, "Whoever died of microbiology?" The name was changed to the Institute of Allergy and Infectious Diseases.[11]

In 1944 the National Cancer Institute was officially classified as a division of NIH and its $700,000 appropriations ceiling was lifted.

[9]Strickland, op. cit., p. 184.
[10]Ibid, p. 2.
[11]Drew, op. cit., p. 78.

Attitudinal Changes Toward Research. In the meantime, an important transformation had taken place in the Congressional attitude toward federal sponsorship of biomedical research. Before WW II, there was a great deal of skepticism among both physicians and politicians as to whether public funds would lead to significant progress in biomedical knowledge. Many felt that only "leaps of genius" would lead to breakthroughs in important research problems, and that these leaps occurred in unpredictable fashion—essentially immune to influence by increases in the supply of personnel or resources. There was also a widely shared persuasion that in the United States there was simply not enough research talent available to absorb adequately major increases in science funding.

But, "the war had a revolutionary effect on medical research."[12] A number of "crash" programs were instituted by the Office of Scientific Research and Development (OSRD) in weapons and medical research relevant to the war effort. The OSRD's Committee on Medical Research operated during this period "under a direct presidential mandate, with a clear purpose and what was tantamount to a blank check."[13] These supercharged medical research efforts proved to be dramatically successful—leading to penicillin, cortisone and steroid development. More importantly, these wartime successes did much to erode the skepticism surrounding public funding for science. In particular,

> Congress was impressed. It attributed the "magnificent progress" in medical research to "adequate financing, coordination and teamwork." And particularly impressive to some Congressmen was how "adequate financing" could speed up conquest of disease and medical problems.[14]

It was this shift in Congressional attitude that was to prove decisive in shaping the future of biomedical research policy. In successive years, Congress was to add new disease divisions to the National Institutes of Health, direct agency attention to those research possibilities that it had become convinced held promise, and upgrade consistently NIH appropriations beyond those levels deemed appropriate by most budget officials of the executive branch and in the agency itself. NIH appropriations grew from $2.8 million at the end

---

[12]"The Steelman Report: Science and Public Policy," as quoted in Penick, J. L., Russell, C. W., Sherwood, M. B., and Swain, D. C. (eds.). *The Politics of American Science, 1939 to the Present* (Chicago: Rand McNally, 1965) p. 109.

[13]Strickland, op. cit., p. 16. For a general treatment of the relationship of science to the federal government during this period, see Greenberg, Daniel S., *The Politics of Pure Science* (New York: New American Library, 1967) Chapters 4 and 5.

[14]Strickland, op. cit., p. 17.

of the war to $2.1 billion by 1972 (the eve of the war on cancer) |107|
under this Congressional tutelage.

This growth in NIH appropriations was not accomplished without substantial tension between Congress and the biomedical research community. Important members of this community, and many NIH officials, despite the wartime experience, did not share Congressional enthusiasm regarding the speed and scale of the disease attack. Many critics charged throughout this growth period that Congress and its research lobby were "force feeding" NIH—pushing the agency into the adoption of unsystematic research projects which, despite their appeal to the popular fancy, were doubtful in terms of scientific yield.

For their part, members of the biomedical lobby and their Congressional advocates believed research policy had to overcome a "small business mentality" native to physicians in order to be successful. This mentality, they believed, imposed an undue conservative restraint upon the outlook of many involved in the biomedical research effort. What was needed instead, it was suggested, was a sense of mission and urgency that would motivate major effort despite cost or risk. For members of the health lobby, research "like any other enterprise, had to be big if big results were to be expected."[15]

It was this "large-scale mentality" of the health lobby that, of course, triumphed in the design and prosecution of biomedical research policy. Despite some reverses—the death, retirement or defeat of key Congressional sponsors, such as Rep. John Fogarty and Senators Lister Hill and Ralph Yarborough, or the well-publicized report in 1967 by the House Intergovernmental Relations Subcommittee that criticized NIH management practices—the large-scale Congressional perspective on health research policy has reigned supreme to the present. It is this perspective that has had a dominant influence on the development of the war on cancer.

The Large-Scale Framework of the War on Cancer

The formal imposition of the large-scale perspective onto cancer research began in 1947. At this time it became clear to officials of the Public Health Service that unless NIH through its cancer institute was prepared to comply with the Congressional will for major research and expenditure acceleration, the agency might well lose preeminence in a major health research area to competing bureaucracies in the executive branch. National Cancer Institute appropri-

¹⁵Ibid., p. 136.

ations suddenly grew dramatically—signalling NIH acquiescence to Congressional policy demands. In 1947, NCI appropriations rose to $1.8 million from the $500,000 of the previous year. In 1948, the rise was more spectacular—to $14.5 million, representing nearly a 700 percent increase.

The cancer attack consisted of grants, contracts and extensive in-house research within NCI. A clinical center was established to treat selected cancer patients in order to advance research. Later, in 1965, an entire set of national cancer, heart disease and stroke centers were approved to offer treatment, research and training facilities in regional locations. By 1970, NCI appropriations had grown to $190 million—the largest of all the health institutes.

This growth reflects relentless pressure applied by the medical research lobby and its Congressional associates. Yet even this level of research commitment and activity proved insufficient for the anticancer advocates. In 1970, Senator Yarborough, as chairman of the Senate Labor and Public Welfare Committee, oversaw the appointment of a National Panel of Consultants on the Conquest of Cancer. This panel was charged with responsibility "to examine the adequacy of . . . support of cancer research, and 'to recommend to Congress and the American people what must be done to achieve cures for the major forms of cancer by 1976—the 200th anniversary of the founding of this great Republic'."[16]

The idea of the panel, as well as its composition, was heavily influenced by Mary Lasker and the medical research lobby. Not surprisingly (as its very charge would seem to compel, in fact) the scientists and laymen of the panel concluded that it was appropriate to upgrade dramatically the nation's anticancer effort. To this end the panel recommended major increases in research appropriations, the construction of 20 new regional cancer centers and the creation of a special agency to oversee it all—an agency independent of NIH which would report directly to the President.[17]

In making these recommendations, the panel appeared to subscribe heavily to the "space program approach" to policy making. It had concluded that "breakthroughs in cancer are imminent, and that given enough money and the proper management techniques, man can conquer cancer just as he has split the atom and landed on the moon."[18]

As a result of the panel's report, legislation was introduced in the Congress to implement its proposals. Senator Yarborough intro-

[16]Ibid., p. 260.
[17]Eisenberg, Lucy, The politics of cancer, Harpers, 243 (November 1971): 105.
[18]Ibid., p. 100.

duced a Conquest of Cancer Act barely one week after the Consultants' report had been made public. Sensing a political groundswell
on behalf of a major anticancer initiative, President Nixon "person-
ally reopened the budget of the National Institutes of Health in early
January 1971—to the particular amazement of the NIH
directorate—and added to the figure his lieutenants had set an extra
$100 million for 'an intensive campaign to find a cure for cancer'."[19]
In his State of the Union address shortly thereafter, Nixon attempted to strengthen his identification with the anticancer cause. Again
in the language of the space program, the President asserted that:

> ... the time has come in America when the same kind of concen-
> trated effort that split the atom and took man to the moon should be
> turned toward conquering this dread disease. Let us make a total na-
> tional commitment to achieve this goal.[20]

Meanwhile, the President and Congress continued to vie for political supremacy in the leadership of the anticancer crusade. Six days
after the President's address, Senators Kennedy and Javitz rein-
troduced the Conquest of Cancer Act into the new Congress (Yarborough had lost his Senate seat in the 1970 elections). The new
legislative proposal, as before, called for the creation of a National
Cancer Authority as an independent agency whose director and
deputy administrator would be appointed by and report directly to
the President. The National Cancer Institute would be absorbed into
the new agency, and a National Cancer Advisory Board, consisting
of nine scientists and nine laymen, would replace the National
Cancer Advisory Council.[21]

While the Congress debated the merits of this proposal, the President was still attempting to assert his leadership over the anticancer
groundswell. In May of 1971, the President offered his own war on
cancer plan, designed to retain some degree of NIH jurisdiction over
the new anticancer initiative. In October, the President ordered the
transformation of Fort Detrick in Maryland, the army's principle
biological warfare research facility, into a cancer research laboratory.

In the end, the War on Cancer Act of 1971 reflected a compromise
between Presidential and Congressional interests but, more importantly, it reflected in most respects the large-scale escalation demands of the biomedical research lobby. The act placed the National
Cancer Institute at the head of the new crusade, but with its budget

[19].Strickland, op. cit., p. 264.
[20]Public Papers of the Presidents: Richard M. Nixon, 1971 (Washington, DC: U.S. Government
Printing Office, 1972) p. 53.
[21]Strickland, op. cit., p. 264.

and director to be determined directly by the President instead of the director of NIH. A three-member President's Cancer Panel was established to review regularly the prosecution of the cancer war from a scientific and management perspective. A National Cancer Advisory Board was also created to offer periodic advice and scrutiny. Finally, the act authorized $1.59 billion to the new effort for a three-year expenditure.[22]

As a result of the new declaration of war, a vastly more comprehensive framework was imposed upon cancer research activities. A Cancer Control Program was added to the responsibilities of NCI in order to diffuse research findings into health care practice by means of education and training. In addition, the war was to be conducted under a project management system patterned after that of the space program. In 1971 and 1972, 250 clinicians and laboratory scientists met in a series of planning sessions to map the direction and specialized activities of the new cancer program. As a result, the war was expressed in terms of a "National Cancer Plan" with seven major objectives ranging from identification of the causes and processes of the disease to the improvement of rehabilitation of cancer patients. These objectives are linked to "program approaches," approach "elements" and project areas in a "strategic plan." In addition, an "operational plan" was developed detailing the specific research programs to be undertaken in support of the war's objectives.[23] A final component in the new cancer initiative was a major program in facilities construction. The cancer act permitted the building of 15 Comprehensive Cancer Centers throughout the country for the extension of research and patient care. A 1974 amendment to the act enlarged this number.

Policy Scale and Cancer Research

The development of the war on cancer represents the encapsulation of a policy objective within the framework of large-scale politics and organization. To be sure, in comparison with such pursuits as manned space exploration, the genesis of the war is decidedly different. It was not, after all, an executive-centered policy, designed and subsequently protected by a politically self-contained bureaucracy. Instead, the war on cancer was a policy derived from Congressional and interest group design. It had its origin in the very institutions that proved so threatening to space policy makers. Yet, despite

[22]Ibid., p. 287.
[23]For a detailed review of war on cancer objectives, see *The National Cancer Program: The Strategic Plan* (Washington, DC: D.H.E.W., 1973).

these differences, the political and administrative environment that came to surround both policies appears much the same.

Both pursuits were cast in terms of major national commitments to objectives with *collectively* derivable benefits: national security and prestige on the one hand and reduction of the threat of a dread disease on the other. Both policies featured substantial appropriations acceleration and a heavy emphasis on facilities construction. Both were conducted under the rubric of project management and master plans.

Most importantly, perhaps, both space exploration and the war on cancer were politically insulated from the conventional policy processes of jurisdictional competition, fragmentation of plans and piecemeal program implementation in the face of scarce resources. In the case of space exploration it was Presidential prestige, the binding nature of an explicit national goal, and the political and technical advantages of a large executive bureaucracy that served to protect the policy, at least for many important years, from disaggregation by Congressional intrusion or from the undermining effects of shifts in public opinion regarding space flight expenditures.

In the development of the war on cancer, it was the *arousal* of Congress, the psychology of dread disease, and the adroit maneuvering of the biomedical research lobby that protected the emerging program from forces of disaggregation *present in the executive branch*. In both cases, the end result was the same—a policy objective surrounded by a large-scale political and resource framework; that is, an environment that largely shielded policy plans and decisions from conventional incremental processes of competition, adjustment and fragmentation.

It is essential to inquire, however, whether the policy *objective* of the war on cancer is, in fact, large-scale—that is, is it truly characterized by the existence of indivisible components among its requisites as was the space program, the policy that the architects of the war sought so self-consciously to emulate. It is on this very question that serious disagreement and controversy have, from its beginnings, surrounded the war.

One source of publicly expressed misgivings concerning the political and administrative framework of the cancer effort has been the biomedical research community itself. Many cancer researchers do not share the large-scale philosophy underlying the war. From the beginning, they have

> ... felt uncomfortable with a goal that was at once so specific and grandiose. Of course finding answers to the affliction of disease was the ultimate hope. But there were more immediate problems to be

attacked carefully, systematically, step by step. The policy goals of the medical research enterprise that was being built therefore should not be stated in such dramatic terms. The basic problem of knowledge gaps must be the goal directly and immediately focused upon; more had to be discovered about genetics, biochemistry, molecular biology, biophysics, immunology. Then on to the next level of understanding, and the next, and the next, in the biosciences. Subsequently, when the knowledge base was sufficient, when understanding of its critical components became finely honed, then a major, focused attack on specific diseases could be mounted with reasonable expectation of success.[24]

The reservations of the research community regarding the war have emerged in many forms. At the outset of the political mobilization on behalf of the war (the release of the National Panel of Consultants' Report to the Congress) an editorial in *Science* cautioned that "the likely result of a . . . crash program is wreckage of the nation's medical research enterprise without much counterbalancing progress in coping with cancer."[25] One prominent researcher publicly asserted that "an all-out effort to cure cancer at this time might be like trying to land a man on the moon without Newton's laws of motion."[26] In 1973, a prestigious committee of the Institute of Medicine of the National Academy of Sciences expressed serious reservations in its review of the National Cancer Plan. In fact, the committee was uneasy with the very concept of the plan.

> Much is said about the lines of research that appear most promising today . . . but too little acknowledgement is made of the genuine possibility that any or all of today's leads, including all of those proposed by the 250 scientists . . . could turn out to be the wrong leads.

> [The plan] leaves the impression that all shots can be called from a central headquarters; that all, or nearly all, of the really important ideas are already in hand, and that given the right kind of administration and organization, the hard problems can be solved. It fails to allow for the surprises which must surely lie ahead if we are really going to gain an understanding of cancer.[27]

The Cancer Research Problem. Underlying these misgivings concerning the war is a critically important research issue. Is the "state-of-the-art" for the conquest of cancer appropriately matched

[24]Strickland, op. cit., p. 188.

[25]*Science* 172 (April 2, 1971).

[26]Spiegelman, Dr. Sol, as quoted in Carlson, Rick J., *The End of Medicine* (New York: J. Wiley, 1975) p. 75.

[27]Culliton, Barbara J., National cancer plan: The wheels and issues go round, *Science* 179 (March 30, 1973): 1306.

to a large-scale political mobilization, comprehensive planning and free-flowing resources? Is the "technology" associated with cancer research, in other words, truly analogous to that of the space program at the time of its acceleration?

Cancer, many researchers would contend, is a uniquely complex "genetic engineering" disease. It is a disease with the power to alter the structure of a cell and to transmit genetically new organizing and behavioral information to subsequent cells. As such, cancer may well be governed by processes *fundamental to life itself.*

The point in this is that we are currently a long way from such fundamental understanding. The fields of molecular biology, biophysics, genetics and immunology at present lack the findings and perhaps even the analytical frameworks to generate these insights. Under these circumstances, successful approaches to cancer inquiry can scarcely be anticipated. If this is so, the large-scale organizational framework that surrounds the war may be wholly inappropriate to cancer research; it may even, in fact, have the potential to undermine such research.

Consider the planning and managerial aspects of the war. As Frank Rauscher, former director of the National Cancer Institute, described it: "The development and coordination of the National Cancer Program involves, first, the *development of a consensus* among clinicians and laboratory scientists about the direction, content, and pace of the research program. [emphasis added].[28] Such consensus was the purpose of the National Cancer Plan and the consultations leading to it. The plan entails research areas of current promise worthy of expanded pursuit. But, of importance, no consensus can foresee or evaluate potentially productive paths hitherto unexplored. In fact, concensus may well discourage the research independence necessary for the exploration of those novel approaches that may have unanticipated yield.

The problem posed by the cancer plan is reminiscent of the dilemma associated with the governance of pure research in general. It is a dilemma well expressed by Albert Hirschman and Charles Lindblom in their argument against "attempts at integrating various subsystems into a well-articulated, harmonious general system" by means of overcontrol or anticipation.[29] Highly complex, uncertain or indeterminate problems that may well exceed existing problem-

[28]*National Cancer Program: Report of the Director, January, 1973* (Washington, DC: D.H.E.W., 1973) p. 4.

[29]Hirschman Albert O., and Lindblom, Charles E., "Economic Development, Research and Development, Policy-Making: Some Converging Views," in *Systems Thinking,* edited by F.E. Emery (Baltimore: Penguin Books, 1972) p. 354.

solving capacities are best resolved, they contend, by flexible and essentially reactive processes rather than by comprehensive, goal-seeking ones. The latter modes of problem-solving threaten greater imbalance and waste in the long run. Scientific research is itself organized around complex issues of great uncertainty and disagreement, and many have asserted that problem-solving processes in science can suffer under rigid systems of anticipation and control.[30]

In the case of cancer research, some critics see identical dangers in the planning and managerial framework of the war. By detailing research objectives in areas of current promise, the plan may divert attention *and resources* from research activities whose link to advances in oncology (the study of cancer) may at present be less certain but whose impact may prove to be substantial.

The systems analytic approach of the cancer plan also troubles some members of the biomedical research community. It implicitly promotes an optimizing strategy with rigidity insofar as scientific risk taking is concerned.[31] This strategy may well come to dominate the grant and contract-awarding decisions taken by the cancer institute.

In addition, the managerial framework established in support of the cancer plan has aroused some scientific suspicions. It stresses a centralization and coordination of the war that some fear will place management personnel in positions to preempt scientific direction of the program. Already one NCI program director has resigned, stating that "a fundamental reason . . . is his belief that active scientists have very little voice in setting policy or priorities in the division of the NCI, and that the division is being run by managers with the help of scientists rather than the other way around."[32] This same scientist contends that "There seems to be a growing gap between the top policy-making decisions of the institute and the expertise which is needed to make these complicated value judgments."[33]

Another large-scale component of the war—finance—has been the target of research critics. Some have contended that given present understanding, further advances against cancer depend primarily upon breakthroughs in basic research—breakthroughs which do indeed depend upon "intuitive leaps of genius" unresponsive in

---

[30]See, for example, Polanyi, Michael, The republic of science: Its political and economic theory, *Minerva* 1, (1) (Autumn, 1962): 54–73; and Polanyi, *The Logic of Liberty* (Chicago: University of Chicago Press, 1951). For an excellent analysis of the implications of science as an autonomous system see Blissett, Marlan, *Politics in Science* (Boston: Little, Brown, 1972) Chapters 2 and 3.

[31]See Culliton, op. cit., pp. 1305–1307.

[32]Wade, Nicholas, Cancer institute: Expert charges neglect of carcinogenesis studies, *Science* 192 (May 7, 1976): 529.

[33]Ibid., pp. 529–530.

their timing to financial saturation.[34] Still others fear that large- |115|
scale funding may introduce major distortions in the organization of
biomedical research. Large (and highly prestigious) sums of money
available for applied research projects of immediate relevance to the
cancer program may divert talent away from pure research in less
favored but potentially important problem areas. The rapid pace of
expenditure increases engendered by the war also raises the specter
in some minds of diminished quality among research and program
personnel. The argument here runs that research positions and funding will rise out of proportion to qualified recipients, resulting in an
increase in careless and lower quality research output.[35]

Finally, uneasiness within the biomedical community centers
around the large-scale political framework of the war. The highly
politicized adoption of anticancer objectives as a "total national
commitment" has placed relentless pressure and scrutiny upon
much of the biomedical research enterprise. Demands for research
results and their immediate application permeate the cancer program and its relations with the Congress. The media hungrily de-
vour any prospective research advances, no matter how tentatively
suggested, raising public expectations that must frequently be dis-
pelled quickly by public disclaimers from embarrassed researchers.[36]

It is within this political environment that critics fear major distortions in the research integrity of the war could easily occur. Political requisites threaten to intrude themselves into the assessment of
research priorities, if not the evaluation of the research itself. Those
who argue along these lines are quick to cite a major chemotherapy
program conducted within NIH as an illustration of the potential
danger.

Begun in 1956 under Congressional pressure (and despite the opposition of many NIH officials), the program screened essentially at
random a wide assortment of compounds for possible cancer remis-
sion effects. Some important advances in cancer control resulted
from this research, but at the same time the program has drawn
consistent complaints that the drug screening was done in an unsystematic (and, at times, inconclusive) way and that some of its ex-

[34]See Silver, George A., Money won't solve everything, Nation 213 (4) (August 16, 1971):
110–114.

[35]Eisenberg, op. cit., p. 104.

[36]Apparently public and organizational pressure for positive cancer research findings has led to
at least one case of the deliberate falsification of research results. This occurred at the prestigious
Sloan-Kettering Cancer Center. For a dramatic account of this incident, see Hixson, Joseph, The
Patchwork Mouse: Politics and Intrigue in the Campaign to Conquer Cancer (New York: Anchor
Press, 1976).

penditures (over $500 million by 1971) might have been distributed more productively to fundamental research. NIH officials themselves have termed the results of the chemotherapy program "dramatic, if limited."[37]

The chemotherapy program, however one might evaluate its contributions, offers illustration of the degree to which the conduct of research is susceptible to political influence. Within the large-scale framework of the war, this influence truly becomes a critical issue. Given the national commitment approach to the policy, the intensity of political pressure has been heightened. In addition, the complexity and comprehensiveness of the war is such that it is rendered highly vulnerable to distortions in the relative pace and scale of its component parts. As former NCI Director Rauscher has noted, for an enterprise as complex as the cancer program:

> ... a major issue ... is balance, in terms of clinic versus laboratory; short-term versus long-term; academic versus commercial; targeted versus nontargeted; grants versus contracts versus intramural; national versus international, and the like.[38]

But, dangerously as Rauscher himself admitted: "Things other than science contribute to this balance."[39]

Policy Scale and Research Consequences

For many, governmental intervention in research, within a large-scale political framework, is an appropriate means to accelerate knowledge and at the same time guarantee its direction toward socially beneficent ends. Certainly for some research problems and the policies that surround them, large-scale and comprehensive government intrusions are indeed appropriate. This, after all, is precisely the assertion we have been repeatedly making in connection with manned space exploration. Yet, in many respects, fundamental differences exist between the requisites of the space program and those of the war on cancer.

The space program was constructed around what were basically engineering issues. The technology of exploration was based upon a foundation of well-established theory in physics, astronomy and astronautics. This was a body of theory on which there existed a great

---

[37]Strickland, op. cit., p. 254.

[38]Rauscher, Frank J. Jr., Budget and the national cancer program, *Science* 184 (May 24, 1974): 875.

[39]Idem. For a recent exploration of the politics involved in the design of the cancer program, see Rettig, Richard A., *Cancer Crusade: The Story of the National Cancer Act of 1971* (Princeton: Princeton University Press, 1977).

deal of corroborating evidence and deep-seated scientific
consensus—much of it longstanding.[40] In fact, the theoretical "capital" for the lunar landing enterprise was really developed in the
1920s and 1930s in the liquid-fueled rocketry research of men such
as Robert Goddard, Konstantin Tsiolkovsky and Hermann Oberth.

But the "technology" of cancer control seems hardly analogous.
Indeed, the major issues associated with the war on cancer are not
truly technological at all: they are scientific. At present, in other
words, the major obstacle to advances in the cure and prevention of
cancer in its various forms is an absence of understanding of the
basic genetic and immunological processes surrounding the disease.
Relevant underlying principles are not conclusively known; there is
no consensus within the scientific community on plausible theories
concerning them.

It is possible to escalate a technological capacity by means of a
large-scale political and resource framework—*if its conceptual
foundation is secure.* But, in the absence of such a foundation, no
technology, irrespective of political enthusiasm, will advance much
beyond its moorings in basic science.

The casting of cancer research into a large-scale framework
threatens not simply to waste resources and raise public expectations prematurely. The real danger is that the framework of the war
might actually *undermine* the very advances in basic research upon
which cancer solutions might ultimately depend. This is so because
the secondary characteristics of the large-scale enterprise are precisely those to which biomedical research is presently unsuited.

The comprehensive planning generally associated with large-
scale projects induces a rigidity of focus and, as we have noted in
the space program, relatively inflexible "go/no-go" decisions in
which major investments of resources and prestige are jeopar-
dized with even minor modifications. Cancer research, on the
other hand, confronts substantial theoretical indeterminacy. Under
these circumstances, wide ranges of administrative flexibility—
regarding program emphasis and funding—would seem decidedly
appropriate. It is distinctly possible, given present knowledge, that
research breakthroughs may eventually occur in areas unforeseeable
by even the most farsighted plan.

The consolidation of programs and their finance, which also ac-
companies a large-scale political and organizational framework, is
equally troubling. Space policy acceleration, it will be remembered,

---

[40]For an insightful discussion of the importance of consensus in the conduct of science, see
Ziman, John, *Public Knowledge: An Essay Concerning the Social Dimensions of Science* (London: Cambridge University Press, 1968).

involved the acquisition by NASA of many diverse research and development programs throughout the armed services, as well as the establishment of one major executive jurisdiction over all civilian space-related operations. Ultimately, NASA appropriations came to account for the dominant share of all research funds spent on space by the federal government. (In this connection, an absence of similar consolidation was asserted to be an important scale deficiency of the war on poverty.)

The National Cancer Act of 1971 outlined the "national cancer program" to be directed by NCI. The cancer institute was at the same time given the charge of coordinating the cancer-related activities of other institutes of health, other federal agencies (such as the Atomic Energy Commission, National Science Foundation and Veterans Administration), state and local governments, private institutions and industry. Clearly NCI does not at present have actual administrative powers to direct these external cancer research and control undertakings, but its role in their design and funding is projected to increase.[41] In addition, the NCI component in total cancer research and control expenditures has been increasing. Although external cancer-related spending is difficult to determine precisely, it is estimated by war on cancer officials that in FY1971, the start of the war, NCI expenditures amounted to 45 percent of all cancer research and control spending in the United States. By FY1973 that share had risen to 57 percent. By 1978 it was over 70 percent.[42] Cancer program officials additionally estimate that the present number of research personnel (approximately 5,000) will have to increase to about 11,000 by FY1982. This requirement will be significant in relation to the total available biomedical research manpower pool projected for that date.[43] The fulfillment of war on cancer personnel demands, even with additional training programs, will likely involve substantial infringement upon the available supply of biomedical research personnel, and particularly those personnel of highest quality.

The war on cancer, in other words, can be expected to influence directly major amounts of research done within the biomedical community. It is likely to substantially divert resources, prestige, and personnel from the remainder. This degree of cancer research monopolization raises distinctly the possibility of a reduction in the number of divergent research perspectives which can be brought to

---

[41]See National Cancer Program: The Strategic Plan, op. cit., pp. III-1 to III-14.

[42]National Cancer Program: Analysis of the Mid-Range Resource Requirements for the National Cancer Program (Washington, DC: U.S. Government Printing Office, 1973) p. A-15.

[43]Ibid., pp. I–11 to I–14.

bear on the cancer problem. The prospects for this reduction exist at |119|
the very time when no one can determine conclusively the research
directions from which cancer breakthroughs are likely to occur.

Cancer Research and Policy Pluralism

The analysis undertaken here of the war on cancer does not obviously lead to the conclusion that dramatic research breakthroughs
will not occur within the present large-scale framework. Some
members of the biomedical research community indeed are convinced that they are likely *only* within such a framework.[44] Further,
it has been aruged, in support of the war, that even without major
research breakthroughs simple refinement of present treatment
techniques and the establishment of a closer program link between
them and the delivery of cancer care will save many lives. This
savings in lives, it is argued, will more than offset waste and mis-
targeted efforts in the cancer program.

The argument here, however, is that in some important respects,
short-run gains under the present policy framework may seriously
delay more substantial advances against cancer in the long run. In
addition, it is possible to upgrade cancer care delivery without re-
sorting to large-scale political and resource mobilizations against
the disease. Merging basic biomedical research, applied cancer research and cancer control programs within the same tightly structured framework might do violence to the first without necessarily
being essential for the latter.

In fact, what may well serve the anticancer cause most effectively
is the recognition that it is in all likelihood a policy objective
small-scale in its requirements. Earlier, those indivisibilities implicit in both space and antipoverty policy objectives have been
elaborated. These indivisibilities, although different in nature, required the support and protection which only large-scale political
frameworks could provide. Indivisible objectives are exceedingly
vulnerable to the ever-present forces of disaggregation associated
with conventional policy frameworks.

But the objectives of the war on cancer appear most likely to be
served *by the very process of disaggregation.* Here is a policy for
which pluralism seems at present decidedly appropriate. Independent and diverse research projects have the potential to expand the
theoretical base of many biomedical fields. Much of this intellectual
capital might well interact in surprising ways to advance the attack

[44]See, for example, Cohen, Seymour S., Cancer research and the scientific community, *Science*
172 (June 18, 1971): 1212–1214.

against cancer.[45] At the same time, cancer control programs could be pursued within a separate organizational arrangement that permits rapid and extensive diffusion of new medical knowledge, but protects basic research from many of the relevancy assessments and scheduling demands appropriate primarily to cancer care delivery.[46]

All of this is not to suggest that substantial sums of money will not, in any form, advance the purposes behind the war on cancer. Even the most basic biomedical research, following the trend of "big science" has become personnel- and equipment-intensive. But care must be taken in the funding of this research to maintain sufficient program disaggregation to cope with the dimensions of uncertainty that presently surround the cancer problem.

It is to be hoped that in the near future a foundation of knowledge will be established that bears directly upon human cancers and their origins. A large-scale and comprehensively targeted attack on the disease based on this understanding might then yield dramatic gains against this most dreaded of pathologies.

[45]This is, after all, the very process upon which major scientific advances and their technological extensions are based. See Meier, Richard L. Analysis of the social consequences of scientific discovery, *American Journal of Physics* 25 (9) (December, 1957): 602–613.

[46]Arguments along this line may be found in Thomas, Lewis, "On the Planning of Science," in *Biomedical Scientists and Public Policy*, edited by H. Hugh Fudenberg and Vijaya Melnick (New York: Plenum Press, 1978) pp. 67–75.

Large-Scale Policy:
An Analytical Perspective

It is appropriate to review briefly the basic elements in the theory of large-scale policy. The roots of the theory lie both in the content of policy objectives and in the "mechanics" of the policy-making process.

At the center of attention are those technological, psychological, organizational and political components or instrumentalities required for the pursuit of given objectives. These policy requirements derive from a number of factors. They may be imposed by the technical or causal nature of a policy problem itself. They may inhere in technological or administrative "states of the art" or in a general consensus as to the way things "should be done." Additionally, specific requisites are frequently imposed by the "logic" of the particular policy design that has been chosen for pursuit of a given objective.

For the manned space exploration program, the nature of the technical problem, the theoretical consensus and the engineering state of the art all dictated special policy-making requisites associated with a lunar landing. For the war on poverty, there was no consensus on the nature of the poverty problem or on the "technology" of antipoverty action. But the design of the war, however arbitrarily arrived at, contained its own set of special requisites. It is important to remember that the analysis of requisites associated with a particular policy design need imply no assessment of the "rightness" of the design itself.

The next element in the theory of large-scale policy derives from a comparative examination of the requisites for diverse sets of policy objectives. For most objectives, it is evident that policy components can be provided in fluctuating amounts, with advancements in policy output (both symbolic and tangible) following these fluctuations in a more or less proportionate relationship. These policy pursuits, in other words, are flexible: their requirements can be pieced together in a variety of ways, at varying levels of intensity or quantity, to provide a range of outputs. Since requisites and payoffs can be made available in these flexible amounts, conventional policy objectives are appropriately matched to the negotiation and adjustment processes native to pluralism.

But, a class of policy objectives exists for which the feasibility characteristics are far different. These objectives present a case in which one or more technological, psychological, organizational or political requirements are not available in flexible or continuous amounts. Instead, owing to the nature of the objective or a special characteristic of the political system, or both, policy-making requisites and the payoffs that depend upon them are derivable only in large and discontinuous "lumps."

This trait poses a fundamental contrast to conventional policy. When even one policy-making requirement can only be provided in "quantum" amounts, the combinational possibilities by which *all* policy requisites can fit together become sharply limited. A prescriptive technology for example, if required, demands large and inflexible amounts of money and personnel. Such resources may in turn demand an extensive political mobilization and an organizational psychology conducive to long-term commitment, short-term sacrifice and high levels of risk taking. For large-scale objectives, the lowest common denominator possible among policy-making requisites can thus be very "large" indeed. These are objectives for which technically plausible and politically sustainable policy pursuits come only at high levels of resource commitment and output. It is in this distinctive sense that we define such objectives as *large-scale*.

Large-scale policy pursuits are, by their very nature, ill-suited to pluralist political processes. These are processes of disaggregated, piecemeal resource application, entailing narrow and uncertain political commitments. Such an environment does not easily accommodate the rigidity of large-scale objectives. Critical mismatches, in fact, occur when large-scale objectives are pursued within pluralist political and organizational frameworks. These mismatches can result in very low, if not politically unacceptable, levels of goal-seeking performance.

On the Comparison of Public Policies

Before discussing the implications of the theory of scale for the study of public policy, it is important to consider the nature of the evidence so far presented. The analysis offered has centered around manned space exploration, with brief comparative investigations of the war on poverty and the war on cancer.

It is immediately apparent that these policies differ in a multitude of important respects. Obviously, the technologies associated with each varied significantly.[1] Space exploration was a technology-intensive policy whose primary objective was the development and engineering of spacecraft hardware. The war on cancer has entailed much more basic research on a much different order of problem. The poverty program operated within an area singularly devoid of technology, well-established scientific theory, or even agreement on the definition of the poverty problem itself.

The clientele associated with each policy were also highly diverse. They ranged from the highest to the lowest end of the social continuum in education, prestige and political power.

Finally, and perhaps most importantly, the policies treated in this analysis have had fundamental differences in the intrinsic property of their goals. Space policy entailed the construction of physical and highly visible technological systems. The war on cancer involves not the contrivance of a visible system but the understanding of a preexisting and highly elusive one. The war on poverty meanwhile was directed toward the manipulation of the system of social opportunity—a system at once all pervasive but vaguely defined and subject to multiple perceptions.

In light of these important distinctions among the policies treated in this analysis, relating them to one another by means of a theory of scale would seem a hazardous undertaking. Comparison, after all, implies some degree of equivalency in those dimensions chosen for the analysis of two or more policies.[2]

[1]For an important treatment of technology types and their effects upon organizational structure, see Thompson, James D., *Organizations in Action* (New York: McGraw-Hill, 1967). See also Mohr, Lawrence B., Organizational technology and organizational structure, *Administrative Science Quarterly* 16(4) (December, 1971): 444–459.

[2]For an insightful treatment of the comparison of policies see Nelson, Richard R., *The Moon and the Ghetto* (New York: Norton, 1977).

It is indeed appropriate to recognize the diversity of those elements that comprise the structure of various policies. But the comparisons offered here are based not upon the intrinsic nature of these elements but rather upon their characteristics of availability and supply. It is the *indivisibility* of policy components and not the policy components *themselves* that we are, comparing.

The use of indivisibility as a comparative concept does not imply that these policy components that defy disaggregation will be the same for every policy. But indivisibility, irrespective of its sources, imposes constraints on policy and affects the conduct in ways that may well be equivalent between policy areas and across policy systems. It is a means, in other words, to relate even highly disparate policies analytically to one another.

Moreover, the divisibility/indivisibility dimension is a truly important policy variable. As we have seen throughout this analysis, the divisibility of policy resources and payoffs can affect in dramatic ways the behavior and performance of policy-making organizations within their political environments. Large-scale policies, in particular, pose major challenges to both policy analysis and the design of policy-making systems.

Scale and Policy Decision Making

One challenge posed by large-scale indivisible policy relates directly to decision making. Large-scale policy objectives require for their pursuit decisions which reflect processes which cannot be accounted for within the prevailing decision model of incrementalism.[3]

Because policy requisites and outputs cannot be provided in continuous quantities, major "go/no-go" decisions must be taken if large-scale policies are to approach politically acceptable levels of goal-seeking performance. These go/no-go decisions are ones that will permit neither the short-term commitment nor the continual adjustment that the incremental model prescribes. Once undertaken, they resist even marginal redefinition of basic objectives. Further, for the organizational system which surrounds a go/no-go decision, marginal shifts, if they did occur, would have far-reaching rather than incremental consequences.

Manned space exploration, as a large-scale policy, well illustrates the deficiencies of the incremental model. It was an objective that

[3]For a description of the provisions of incrementalism, see, again, Lindblom, Charles E., The 'science' of muddling through, *Public Administration Review* 19 (2) (Spring, 1959): 79–88. For a discussion of alternatives to the incremental model of decision making, see Etzioni, Amitai, *The Active Society* (New York: The Free Press, 1968) esp. Chapter 12. Also suggestive of the limits of incrementalism is Rose, Richard, Models of governing, *Comparative Politics* 51 (4) (July, 1973): 465–496.

required for its pursuit a comprehensive commitment to the Kennedy lunar landing goal. It was certainly a policy for which no prec-
edent existed, and its decisions could not be based (as incrementalism specifies) on "limited comparisons to those policies . . . presently in effect."[4]

Those start-up requirements associated with large-scale policy
objectives represent significant departures from the assumptions of
the incremental model. Comprehensive investment must be made
in planning and organizing a large-scale policy effort before any significant payoffs are derived. The indivisibility of the large-scale policy objective means, in effect, that it is beset by critical thresholds in
the "curve" of its performance. Below these thresholds, incremental
additions to an "underscaled" policy are not likely to lead to proportionate gains in output performance. The efforts of the Eisenhower
administration to upgrade space exploration capabilities of the
United States, for example, had minimal payoffs because key research and facilities construction thresholds had not yet been
reached.

Beyond threshold points, however, incremental increases to policy requisites can yield vastly multiplied gains in performance.
Dramatic changes can occur suddenly and discontinuously under
the impact of forces that can establish themselves only at a specific
scale of operation. It is precisely this kind of relationship, for example, that underlies Rostow's notion of a "take-off" point for national
economic growth.[5]

Threshold phenomena are poorly understood throughout the social sciences, yet they are highly important to the understanding of a
great many social processes. As Kenneth Boulding has observed:

> [Social] depreciation and appreciation are not continuous functions of
> use or load, but exhibit threshold or overload phenomena, which is
> what causes crises. . . . Continuous functions, which are fine for celes-
> tial mechanics, are characteristic of social mechanics only over small
> ranges of variation, and most social problems arise because of discon-
> tinuous functions—the road that suddenly jams up as one more car
> appears on it, the river that refuses to clean itself under a single addi-
> tion of sewage, the internationl system that breaks down into war, or
> the city that erupts into riot when some small straw is laid onto some
> existing back.[6]

[4]Lindblom, op. cit., p. 84.
[5]See Rostow, W. W., *The Stages of Economic Growth* (Cambridge: Harvard University Press,
1971) esp. pp. 36–58.
[6]Boulding, Kenneth, Discussion, in The political economy of environmental quality, *American
Economic Review* 61 (2) (May, 1971): 167. For an analysis of public opinion thresholds and their
importance within the context of state policy making, see Hopkins, Anne H., Opinion publics and
support for public policy in the American states, *American Journal of Political Science* 18 (1)
(February, 1974): 167–177.

| 126 | Discontinuities, such as those defined by thresholds, simply defy a smooth gradient of successive goal approximations as postulated by incrementalism. Thresholds render it exceedingly difficult for a series of small incremental steps to add up to a cumulative fashion to one big, comprehensive step. This is a critical weakness in the incremental strategy, and an area where careful attention to large-scale policy is urgently needed. A brief urban policy example may suggest the dimensions of the problem.

Many efforts have been undertaken in the last two decades to renew inner-city areas and promote general urban rejuvenation. It is becoming increasingly evident through these efforts that the reinvigoration of cities represents a policy objective to which thresholds or critical masses are attached. Slums represent resource and structural "sinks"—downward spirals of delapidation and capital depreciation. The influx of limited recovery-inducing elements into the slum environment—in the form of public housing projects, piecemeal slum clearance efforts and private capital investment—is rarely sufficient to overcome the "sink" effect that characterizes the slum. The decay rate of public housing, as well as shrinking inner-city investment returns testify to the failure of small-scale, incremental policy interventions to effect slum rejuvenation.[7]

It seems distinctly possible that only massive efforts, commitments and expenditures will result in a cycle of rejuvenation that could overcome the sink effect and establish itself as self-sustaining. Major capital inflows will begin to justify private inner-city investment. This investment will, in turn, enlarge the urban job market, providing resources and incentives for the repair and rebuilding of slum housing. The subsequent appreciation of this housing will add to the supply of inner-city capital, and so on.[8]

If this is so, as urban redevelopment policy, unless cast on a scale approaching its critical resource thresholds, has little chance of realizing, *or even approximately realizing,* its ends. The potential challenge here to a strategy of incrementalism is unmistakable. A series of small commitments or steps, below a policy threshold, will not advance the policy even incrementally in the direction of its goals. Yet at a critical point of commitment, a "take-off" can occur in policy output, yielding vastly multiplied gains in goal-seeking performance.

[7]For a discussion of the urban decay spiral, see Baumol, William J., Macroeconomics and unbalanced growth: The anatomy of the urban crisis, *American Economic Review* 57 (June, 1967): 415–426. Also Richardson, Harry W., *Urban Economics* (London: Penguin Books, 1971) pp. 133–145.

[8]For an analysis of these potential "accelerator effects" in urban renewal, see Thompson, Wilbur R., *A Preface to Urban Economics* (Baltimore: The Johns Hopkins Press, 1965) pp. 299–302.

Large-Scale Policy and Cybernetic Models. Another decision model equally challenged by the phenomenon of large-scale policy, is the deviance-minimizing, self-regulating system of cybernetics. The cybernetic approach, which has gained great currency recently throughout the social sciences, assumes that decisions represent the operation of a monitoring and self-corrective mechanism which is "honing in" on a given state or objective.[9]

"In order for the system to approach the goal effectively [a] . . . feedback condition must be given. The system must receive information concerning the changes in its distance from the goal brought about by its own performance."[10] Additionally, "The system must be able to respond to this information by changes in its own position or behavior."[11] The cybernetic model describes the operation of radar tracking devices, thermostats, missile guidance systems, and even the regulatory functions of the human body. In a social context, it describes state-maintaining systems that restore or readjust equilibrium after confrontation with elements of turbulence. The monitoring and feedback capability assumed by the cybernetic model allows a variety of systems to successively minimize departures from a steady state within which they are structured to operate.

Yet significantly, large-scale policy objectives and the organizational frameworks appropriate to them depart from the deviance-minimizing, self-stabilizing and equilibrating operations defined by cybernetics. As we have seen, large-scale policy enterprises are frequently deprived, by their own indivisibility, of middle ground between open-ended expansion and organizational decay. Yet this middle ground is precisely the property upon which cybernetics and the other "adjustive" theories of decision making strongly rely. These theories essentially are grounded in notions of equilibrium. They stress the establishment of balances—between bureaucrat and client, between policy activities and public pressure or, as in the case of incrementalism, between bureaucratic decisions of the present and organizational practice in the past.

Equilibrium implies a "steady state owing to the balance of complimentary forces."[12] But large-scale policy is devoid of exactly this steady state. Its indivisibility requirements necessitate political commitments difficult to sustain in a steady state. Large-scale

[9]For a description of the cybernetic model, see Steinbruner, John, *The Cybernetic Theory of Decision* (Princeton: Princeton University Press, 1975) Chapters 2 and 3; Deutsch, Karl W., *The Nerves of Government* (New York: The Free Press, 1966), and Etzioni, op. cit., Chapters 6–12.

[10]Deutsch, op. cit., p. 184.

[11]Idem.

[12]Moore, Wilbert E., *Social Change* (Englewood Cliffs, NJ: Prentice-Hall, 1963) p. 10.

policies, in fact, are *nonequilibrating* with respect to the psychological and resource mobilizations upon which they depend.

Manned space exploration has been the victim of just this instability. In a fashion analogous to social movements, space exploration has had to mobilize continuous public support toward ever-expanding goals or lose the commitment which sustained the policy in the first place.[13] As we have seen, little in the way of balance has been realizable in between. The poverty program too has been subject to wide fluctuations between intensive political activation and public disillusionment. Perhaps a more dramatic illustration of the instability associated with large-scale policy, however, can be found in a radically different setting—the war in Vietnam.

Equilibrium and Escalation in Vietnam. Perhaps no policy pursuit has engendered more critical reappraisal than United States counterinsurgency operations in Vietnam. A great deal has been written about the origins of the American ground forces commitment, its rationality or irrationality, and the political and bureaucratic factors which escalated the commitment over time. No effort will be made here to evaluate the policy; that, after all, is not at issue in the theory of scale. Instead the argument here is that American counterinsurgency policy, because of its large-scale quality, could not be stabilized between states of escalation and withdrawal.

In the spring of 1965, U.S. military strategists were faced with a dilemma. North Vietnamese regular army units were participating in a growing number of military engagements in the South. At the same time, the Saigon government, disorganized by a succession of coups after the assassination of Ngo Dinh Diem, was rapidly losing control of the South Vietnamese countryside. General William Westmoreland, commander of U.S. forces in Vietnam, had concluded and reported to Washington that "the government of Vietnam could not survive this mounting enemy military and political offensive for more than six months, unless the United States chose to increase its military commitment. Substantial numbers of U.S. ground combat forces were required."[14]

By July, the massive commitment of U.S. ground forces began, accompanied by intensified bombing of infiltration and supply lines

---

[13]For a discussion of those problems associated with sustaining public commitments, see Etzioni, op. cit., pp. 257–260.

[14]Westmoreland, General William C., "Report on Operations in South Vietnam: January 1964–June 1968," in *Report on the War in Vietnam* (Washington, DC: U.S. Government Printing Office, 1968) p. 98.

in both North Vietnam and Laos. U.S. troop strength grew from |129| 21,000 "advisers" in 1964 to a peak of 538,000 by 1968.[15]

It is ironic that the objectives behind this major troop deployment were initially quite modest. The military goals involved simply "arresting the losing trend, stifling the enemy initiative, protecting the deployment of our forces, and providing security to populated areas to the extent possible."[16] In essence these themselves were objectives to *stabilize* the situation in Vietnam—to restore the strategic setting to a steady state. Yet these efforts proved to be large-scale in their feasibility. They necessitated policy resources and commitments that could not be provided at intermediate ranges and could not be maintained in a steady state.

The commitment of American forces overseas required domestic political justification. This, in turn, led officials to *oversell* the policy to the American public in grandiloquent terms in order to guarantee the necessary support. As the political scientist Theodore Lowi describes it:

> No policy has escaped injury to itself and to national interests and international stability in the years since American statesmen have felt the need *to oversell policies in order to avoid coming up with a partial decision.* The war in Vietnam has been just another instance of the point. The fighting in the South was not of our making. The crisis was. The escalation was. The involvement in Vietnam was sold by American image-makers as a case of unambiguous aggression and therefore of the need for military victory. Perhaps it was both of these things, but to sell it on the front pages that way in order to ensure support at home left world diplomats, including our own, with almost no options.[17]

As the United States Vietnam engagement proceeded, the full dimensions of its policy requirements began to present themselves. "By mid-1966 a still further escalation of the war was considered necessary to counter the North's response to the previous U.S. escalation."[18] This upward spiral of escalation continued into 1968, at which time the United States had committed over 538,000 ground troops to the conflict. The momentums of the policy had fully established themselves. Critics, during this period, accused the Johnson administration of "following a policy of escalation which is graduated but open-ended."[19]

As it turned out, the level of commitment associated with Viet-

[15]Ibid., p. 197.
[16]Ibid., p. 100.
[17]Lowi, Theodore J., *The End of Liberalism* (New York: Norton, 1968) p. 179.
[18]Kahin, George Mc. and Lewis, John W., *The United States in Vietnam* (New York: Dell, 1969) p. 183.
[19]Ibid., p. 182.

nam policy—still not demonstrably effective—proved impossible to sustain, even within the "national security" framework under which it had been generated. Major military withdrawls ensued, and subsequent events dramatically illustrated the degree to which the U.S. had failed to realize its initial Vietnam policy objectives.

Here again was a large-scale policy objective whose pursuit could not define a resource, political or organizational steady state. This was the nonequilibrating nature of U.S. counterinsurgency operations in Vietnam—*even though those objectives entailed a goal of stabilization.* Large-scale requirements engender just this characteristic in policy. They demand that policy systems grow continually simply because essential policy requisites *are not maintainable without growth.*

Thus, large-scale policy frequently eludes the equilibrium assumptions of the cybernetic (and incremental) model of decision. It resists equilibrating and stabilizing strategies because *it is devoid of the middle ground which would allow such piecemeal or adjustive actions to be successful.* In essence, large-scale policy involves not deviance-minimizing processes of stabilization, but rather far more complex processes of deviance *amplification*—take-offs based upon systems of mutual causation. Entirely new policy-making models may well have to be fashioned to account adequately for deviance-amplifying processes. Yet, as one analyst has suggested:

> Such systems are ubiquitous: accumulation of capital in industry, interpersonal processes which produce mental illness, evolution of living organisms, the rise of cultures of various types, interpersonal conflicts, and the processes that are loosely termed as "vicious circles" and "compound interests"; in short, all processes of mutual causal relationships that amplify an insignificant or accidental "kick," build up deviation and diverge from the initial condition.[20]

New departures in policy and decision analysis would seem appropriate if we are to understand adequately the indivisibility and instability connected with large-scale undertakings. In the meantime, some highly practical implications reside in the theory of large-scale policy.

The Policy Implications

To repeat a theme mentioned at the very outset of this book, we are living through an age of widespread disillusionment. Great skepticism surrounds the assessment of major social institutions and or-

---

[20]Maruyama, Margoroh, "The Second Cybernetics: Deviation-Amplifying Mutual Causal Processes," in *Modern Systems Research for the Behavioral Scientist*, edited by Walter Buckley (Chicago: Aldine, 1968) p. 304.

ganizations. Little enthusiasm exists for the support of large-scale |131|
undertakings in the public sector. We have come to believe that
largeness-of-scale itself may lie at the heart of our most conspicuous
social problems. Large organizations, expansive societal aspirations,
even economic growth itself are subject to increasingly critical
scrutiny.[21] New attention has been focused on the virtues of smallness, self-reliance, and community (as opposed to national) identifi-
cations. As one author has contended eloquently:

> We have delegated all of our vital functions and responsibilities to
> salesmen and agents and bureaus and experts of all sorts. We cannot
> feed and clothe ourselves, or entertain ourselves, or communicate
> with each other, or be charitable or neighborly or loving, or even
> respect ourselves, without recourse to a merchant or a corporation or a
> public service organization or an agency of the government or a style-
> setter or an expert. Most of us cannot think of dissenting from the
> opinions or actions of one organization without first forming a new
> organization.
>
> . . . The lotus-eaters of this era are in Washington, DC, Thinking Big.
> Somebody comes up with a problem, and somebody in the govern-
> ment comes up with a plan or a law. The result mostly has been the
> persistence of the problem, and the enlargement and enrichment of
> the government.
>
> . . . While the government is "studying" and funding and organizing
> the Big Thought, nothing is being done. But the citizen who is willing
> to Think Little, and, accepting the discipline of that, to go ahead on
> his own, is already solving the problem.[22]

On this same theme, economist E. F. Schumacher, in his book,
Small Is Beautiful, describes "an almost universal idolatry of giantism."[23] "We must learn," he contends, "to think in terms of an
articulated structure that can cope with a multiplicity of small-scale
units."[24]

There is an engaging quality to these assertions and, indeed, com-
pelling evidence for many of them. Many policy makers themselves
are at least partially persuaded, and moves have taken place to de-
centralize public programs in the direction of greater citizen participation and community control.[25]

[21]See, for example, Mishan, E. J., *Technology and Growth: The Price We Pay* (New York:
Praeger Publishers, 1971) and Schumacher, E. F., *Small is Beautiful: Economics as if People
Mattered* (New York: Harper and Row, 1975).

[22]Berry, Wendell, "Think Little," in *A Continuous Harmony: Essays Cultural and Agricultural*
(New York: Harcourt, Brace, Jovanovich, 1972) pp. 76 and 80.

[23]Schumacher, op. cit., p. 66.

[24]Ibid., p. 75.

[25]See, in this connection, Kaufman, Herbert, Administrative decentralization and political
power, *Public Administration Review*, 29 (January/February, 1969) : 3–15.

Further, a growing conviction among scholars and politicians alike asserts the necessity "to think more systematically about the virtues of disaggregation vs. integration, pluralism vs. coordination, and the free market vs. regulation in social life."[26] There are frequent calls for a "debureaucratization" of public policy wherein bureaucratic decisions are supplanted by popular decisions (as in citizen participation and community control) and by market decisions (in which a market adjustment of individual preferences, such as in voucher plans, replaces efforts at centralized planning or regulation.)[27]

In this connection, many of the merging trends in the analysis and assessment of public policy lead further in the direction of elevating decentralized, divisible processes as the "stuff" of policy making. The "public choice" school of policy analysis, in particular, applies the small-scale perspective in its assessment of policy activity. This approach in effect assumes the existence of a decision "market" in which the forces of competition, bargaining and exchange are the determining factors in policy output.[28]

Yet the arguments for decontrol and the public choice frameworks of policy making ignore the essential "wholeness" that characterizes large-scale objectives. Large-scale policy represents the pursuit of objectives unfulfillable by a series of individualized, partial and disaggregated steps. Small decisions, however beneficial or rationally constructed they may be within their own context, *will simply not "add up" to a rational large-scale outcome in their aggregate.* This is, in effect, the defining trait of that class of objectives upon which we have been concentrating.

Scale and Decision Rationality. The theory of scale suggests that there are important circumstances under which highly uncertain links exist between individual actions and their collective consequences. Small-scale efforts can fail to yield desired large-scale results. Below a policy threshold, for example, small resource commitments may have negligble impact in the promotion of a large-scale objective. Yet the theory of scale also suggests that at times small decisions may indeed comprise a large-scale outcome—*but an*

[26]Altshuler, Alan, "New Institutions to Serve the Individual," in *Environment and Policy: The Next Fifty Years*, edited by William M. Ewald (Bloomington: Indiana University Press, 1968) p. 425.

[27]Ibid., pp. 437–441.

[28]For representative offerings in the public choice school, see such works as Buchanan, James M. and Tullock, Gordon, *The Calculus of Consent* (Ann Arbor: University of Michigan Press, 1962); Ilchman, Warren F., and Uphoff, Norman T., *The Political Economy of Change* (Berkeley: University of California Press, 1969); and Mitchell, William C., *Public Choice in America* (Chicago: Markham, 1971).

outcome for removal from small-scale intent.[29] It is distinctly pos- sible, in other words, for a series of small, intrinsically rational decisions, such as those likely under conditions of policy decentralization, to add up to an additive irrationality. Precisely this case has been argued by biologist Garrett Hardin in his well-known work, "The Tragedy of the Commons." The pursuit of individual "welfare functions" with respect to family size, he contends, threatens to add up to a collective "tragedy" where world-wide population capacity is concerned.[30]

In another context, economist Alfred Kahn has made a similar argument, describing a "tyranny of small decisions" at work in the national economy. Individually rational market decisions, Kahn asserts, may lead to an aggregate irrationality on a larger scale precisely because they are small decisions shrouded in myopic perspectives.

> It is an inherent characteristic of a consumer-sovereign, market economy that big changes occur as an accretion of moderate-sized steps, each of them the consequence of "small" purchase decisions—small in their individual size, time perspective, and in relation to their total, combined, ultimate effect. Because changes take place in this fashion, it sometimes produces results that conflict with the very values the market is supposed to serve. .... "Large" changes are effected by a cumulation of "small" decisions; ... consumers never get an opportunity to vote with their dollars on the large changes as such; and if they were given the opportunity, they might not approve what they have wrought.[31]

It is distinctly possible in this regard that the public choice policy "consumer," by the very smallness of his decentralized decision, may be condemned to large-scale market outcomes far removed from individualized intent. As Kahn argues, "the consumer can be victimized by the narrowness of the contexts within which he exercises his sovereignty."[32]

There are important policy implications entailed here. Decentralized and public choice approaches to policy making fail conspicuously to cope with large-scale phenomena. These strategies may in themselves contribute to the generation of unanticipated and decidedly unwelcome large-scale consequences. At the same

---

[29]For a cogent theoretical exploration of this phenomenon see Schelling, Thomas C. *Micromotives and Macrobehavior* (New York: Norton, 1978).

[30]Garrett Hardin, The tragedy of the commons, *Science* 162 (December 16, 1968) pp. 1243−1248. See also in this connection Olson, Mancur, *The Logic of Collective Action* (Cambridge: Harvard University Press, 1965).

[31]Kahn, Alfred, The tyranny of small decisions, *Kyklos* 19 (1) (March, 1966): 44−45.

[32]Ibid., p. 24.

time, they undercut the resource and support frameworks necessary to the pursuit of intensely desired social objectives that may, in fact, be large-scale in their feasibility.

The Inapplicability of Trial Programs. One very specific challenge posed in this regard relates to limited-scope "trial" programs in policy making. These programs are frequently employed in policy settings because, in the event of failure, not too much in the way of prestige or organizational resources has been risked in them. If they succeed, they provide a blueprint for adjustments in design and an enlargement of application. These advantages have led many policy makers, in the spirit of decentralization, to urge that we "expand the area of governmental and public affairs activity in which new ideas can be tried out as limited-scale programs."[33] A variety of work incentive and income maintenance "experiments" have been carried out recently under this philosophy.

Yet here again the theory of scale presents itself. Small-scale policy efforts do not necessarily replicate larger ones. Trial programs cannot hope to duplicate those commitment and resource thresholds upon which large-scale objectives must rely. They may fail to indicate the second- and third-order consequences of large-scale policy in operation. As a result, limited-scale programs are likely to be seriously misleading indicators of large-scale policy performance. Such programs may suggest a potential for success which is really mythical where larger forces must come into play. Perhaps of more importance, they may project failure where success is possible, given resource commitments on the requisite scale.

Issues in Policy Guidance and Accountability. Apart from the challenge to trial programs, a host of more fundamental policy-making issues are raised by the theory of large-scale objectives. Consider the basic political strategy of policy-making organizations. These organizations, in most cases, are able to address themselves to objectives which can be politically defined in ways compatible with institutional predispostions and longstanding commitments and coalitions. Policy makers are able to address *pieces* of problems which they are able to attack in isolation from larger causal systems to which they might connect. Thus policy organizations are able to *decompose* a complex issue into simpler and more narrowly focused

---

[33]Yarmolinsky, Adam, "Ideas into Programs," in *The Presidential Advisory System*, edited by Thomas E. Cronin and Sanford D. Greenberg (New York: Harper and Row, 1969) p. 99. For further discussion of experimental policy making see Rivlin, Alice M., *Systematic Thinking for Social Action* (Washington, DC: The Brookings Institution, 1971) pp. 108–119.

ones which permit a stable and politically sustainable attack. Her- |135|
bert Simon has shown in fact that the decomposability or "near-
decomposability" of complexity is at the heart of the design and
evolution of organizations.[34]

Conventional strategies of policy making closely depend upon the
decomposability of public problems or objectives. Decision theorist
Paul Diesing has asserted that for successful policy it is essential "to
select a problem area that is independent enough from the context
to maintain a separate solution against outside pressures."[35] This
strategy, Diesing notes, allows an organization to attack the easiest
parts of a problem first—economizing on risk taking and the commitment of resources—and to enlarge progressively the problem attack over time, while always operating from a stable base.

Yet large-scale objectives defy just such political strategies. They
are *nondecomposable* in the sense that no isolated "chunks" can be
broken off and dealt with independently in either a technically
plausible or politically sustainable way. Large-scale objectives offer
few stable "niches" from which conventional problem-solving
strategies can be launched.

The contrasts between the requirements of large-scale objectives
and the political environment typically surrounding policy making
are both stark and troublesome. The policy environment in democratic societies is highly competitive. Diverse interests struggle for
benefits and specialized bureaucracies strive for initiative and jurisdictional control. It is an environment of conflicting values and
scarce resources.

Within this setting, the large-scale policy objective is exceedingly
burdensome and vulnerable. It requires enormous quantities of resources where their availability is limited. It demands firm commitments where unanimity is all too infrequent. It displays an indivisibility and "wholeness" of design where bargaining and compromise are the order of the day.

Large-scale policies, if pursued within their required resource and
organizational frameworks, display enormously troublesome political characteristics. Frequently these policies will be oversold to the
public to gain the support and resources deemed essential to the
overcoming of thresholds. Once oversold, policy objectives become
rigid—resisting even minor modifications and adjustments because
of the erosion of support which such modifications threaten. For

---

[34]Simon, Herbert A., The architecture of complexity, *Proceedings of the American Philosophi-
cal Society* 106 (December, 1962) : 467–482.
[35]Diesing, Paul, "Noneconomic Decision-Making," in *Organizational Decision-Making* edited
by Marcus Alexis, and Charles Z. Wilson (Englewood Cliffs, NJ: Prentice-Hall, 1967) p. 191.

|136| manned space exploration, the Kennedy lunar landing commitment became the major sustaining but also the major *constraining* factor with which space policy makers had to deal.

At the same time, large-scale organizational frameworks established in support of indivisible policy objectives are in themselves highly unstable—unable to balance themselves between open-ended cycles of growth and downward spirals of decay. Large organizations can enter into tightly interactive, "reflexive" relationships with their environments—establishing self-justifying environmental demands leading to further organizational growth. At the other extreme, the absence of continuing public mobilization undermines the political power necessary simply to sustain organizational resources once they reach critically high levels. To recall former NASA administrator James Webb's contention is appropriate: "Any uncertainty or shortfall in the support factor is apt to have far-reaching effects . . . and force the [large-scale] endeavor into serious difficulties."[36]

All of these characteristics pose challenges to political control and accountability methods practiced in democratic societies. The rigidity of large-scale policy renders it resistant to the compromise and adjustment processes of political bargaining—frequently the major means by which interest representation and public control are imposed.

The requisites of large-scale policy pursuits frequently entail bureaucratic ascendence over legislative and judicial institutions. Bureaucracy alone seems able to provide the resource continuity and planning coherence appropriate to these enterprises, while at the same time protecting them from the processes of disaggregation to which they are exceedingly vulnerable. Yet bureaucratization adds to the rigidity of large-scale policy and places it within a framework from which it can elude legislative oversight and public scrutiny.

Lastly, the instability of large-scale policy directly threatens democratic control capacities. In what ways can societies disengage from rigid, nonincremental policy endeavors that have entered into self-escalating spirals of growth? Disengagement is difficult to accomplish because of heightened aspirations and bureaucratic momentums which support such spirals. If it is accomplished, it can well lead to political turbulence of major dimensions as organizational disintegration and public disillusionment set in. The war in Vietnam would appear to illustrate this disengagement dilemma to a frightening degree.

[36]Webb, James E., *Space-Age Management* (New York: McGraw-Hill, 1969) p. 63.

Given these characteristics, it is not surprising that great cynicism, if not outright hostility, surrounds large-scale public undertakings. Yet, peculiarly, despite these disaffections, interest in expansive *goals* remains. Solutions are still urgently sought to problems of poverty, inflation, unemployment and urban decay. Demands continue for major improvements in transportation, housing, energy supply and environmental quality. Many of these may well prove to be large-scale demands. Yet the public mood as well as decentralization and tax reduction movements may force us to rely for their resolution upon small-scale, disaggregated policy efforts.

In many problem areas, the danger exists that conventional pluralist and incremental policy attempts will fail repeatedly as each falls below some critical effectiveness threshold. Perhaps only large-scale and indivisible modes of policy making will prove to be adequate in the satisfaction of many of our implicit societal aspirations.

What is truly needed is new analytical attention to the phenomenon of large-scale policy. We must find ways to identify, prior to public commitment, which policy objectives are likely to possess indivisibility requirements. This identification might allow for more enlightened political decisions regarding these policies. We need also to learn how to design more congenial political environments, *while maintaining accountability safeguards*, should large-scale policy commitments be undertaken.

In the meantime, there seems to be no easy answer to the dilemma of large-scale public policy. We have come to accept high societal aspirations as appropriate. Yet frequently the policy efforts necessary to realize these aspirations appear to generate their own troublesome and seemingly intractable requirements. Certainly we must come to understand the nature of scale itself if we are ever to achieve an effective reconciliation between our desire to attain large-scale objectives and our reluctance to support large-scale policy undertakings.

Index